Aids for Interpreting
the Lessons of the Church Year

Easter

Robert H. Smith

Series C

FORTRESS PRESS   PHILADELPHIA

Second printing 1989

Library of Congress Cataloging-in-Publication Data

Proclamation 4: aids for interpreting the lessons of the church year /Christopher R. Seitz.

p. cm.

Consists of 28 volumes in 3 series designated A, B, and C, which correspond to the cycles of the three-year lectionary. Each series contains 8 basic volumes with the following titles: Advent/Christmas, Epiphany, Lent, Holy Week, Easter, Pentecost 1, Pentecost 2, and Pentecost 3.

ISBN 0–8006–4153–1

1. Bible—Liturgical lessons, English.   I. Seitz, Christopher R.
BS391.2.S37   1988
264'.34—dc19   88–10982

4076E89   Printed in the United States of America   1-4157

Contents

Introduction 5

The Resurrection of Our Lord
  Easter Day 7

Easter Evening or Easter Monday 15

The Second Sunday of Easter 20

The Third Sunday of Easter 26

The Fourth Sunday of Easter 32

The Fifth Sunday of Easter 37

The Sixth Sunday of Easter 43

The Ascension of Our Lord 48

The Seventh Sunday of Easter 53

The Day of Pentecost 59

Introduction

Luke's Gospel or the Book of Acts provides at least one of the lessons on each of the Sundays or holidays treated in these chapters on the Easter season—and with good reason. God's resurrection of Jesus, God's reaching down into the tomb to thwart the designs of Jesus' enemies, God's wrenching Jesus from the embrace of death and lifting him to life, to the right hand, to power, is the burning center of Luke's spiritual vision.

Jesus' resurrection is at the heart of Christian believing and teaching; and not the birth of Jesus nor even the crucifixion has anything like equal weight. Easter holds a unique place in the Lukan sky. Everything else revolves around it and is held in place by its gravitational power. It can and does stand alone in Luke-Acts as a summary of the Christian proclamation (cf. Acts 4:1–2; 17:18).

For Luke, the resurrection is the central fact in Jesus' story. But beyond that, the resurrection is the center of Scriptures, the center of history, and the center of Jewish hope.

The Scriptures are full of the promise of God's coming victory over all ugliness and sin, and Luke finds the resurrection of Jesus in numerous individual passages as well as in Scripture as a whole.

Devout Jews in Jesus' day disagreed about the precise shape of the prophesied fulfillment. Religious patriots ("zealots") dreamed of the early defeat of Israel's political oppressors and of the restoration of national splendor (Luke 19:11; Acts 1:6). Sadducees (Luke 20:27; Acts 4:1–2; 23:6–10), on the other hand, counted neither on resurrection nor on political rebellion. They were convinced that Israel's glory resided in her temple and ritual and that the health of the people depended on a policy of accommodation with Roman power.

In the Book of Acts, Luke voices a sense of spiritual kinship with the Pharisees, whom he portrays as pacifistic and anti-Sadducean believers in the resurrection (5:33–39; 23:6–10).

The only possible alternatives to the resurrection as the center of Luke's theology are "the kingdom of God" (Luke 4:43; Acts 1:3) or the proclamation of Jesus as "Lord" and "Christ" and "Son" (Acts 2:36; 9:20). And yet these are not alternatives to resurrection. They paraphrase resurrection. God has established the divine sovereignty through the resurrection and has lifted Jesus up to high new status as

Christ and Lord. Jesus now sits upon David's throne, and of his kingdom there will be no end (Luke 1:32–33; Acts 2:30). To recite his royal titles or to announce his sovereignty are ways of explicating the meaning of resurrection.

Acts supplies most of the first readings, and most of the second lessons are from the Book of Revelation. That is fitting, since Revelation in vision after vision declares the final victory of God over death and hurt, and encourages readers, surrounded by emblems of Roman power and by the hostility of pagan neighbors, with the hope of the new heaven and new earth.

The Gospel of John provides eight of the ten Gospel readings for the days under consideration in this volume. Year after year John dominates the Easter season, and with good reason. Every page of John's Gospel portrays the resurrected Jesus, who still bears the marks of suffering love (20:27), as the source of real life (20:31).

According to John, Jesus has come not only to raise Lazarus (chap. 11) but to bestow upon all believers life from above (3:3), eternal life (3:16), life overflowing and abundant (10:10).

Jesus is Bread of Life (6:35), Fresh and New Life (11:25), Living Path (14:6), Tree of Life (15:1, 5). Through him, through his earthly and bodily reality hoisted up on the cross (3:14–15; 12:32), seekers can come into the presence of God. They will know God and be one with God. Death, transitoriness, change, fading, striving, seeking will give way to knowing, having, abiding, and living.

The Resurrection of Our Lord
Easter Day

Lutheran	Roman Catholic	Episcopal	Common Lectionary
Exod. 15:1–11 or Ps. 118:14–24	Acts 10:34, 37–43	Acts 10:34–43 or Isa. 51:9–11	Acts 10:34–43 or Isa. 65:17–25
1 Cor. 15:1–11	Col. 3:1–4 or 1 Cor: 5:6–8	Col. 3:1–4 or Acts 10:34–43	1 Cor. 15:19–26 or Acts 10:34–43
Luke 24:1–11 or John 20:1–9 (10–18)	John 20:1–9	Luke 24:1–10	John 20:1–18 or Luke 24:1–12

Easter sermons too often try to persuade hearers that Jesus really rose from the dead. The lections for Easter assume the truth of his resurrection instead of arguing for it. The authors apply themselves to the task of drawing out the consequences of his resurrection for the lives of their readers.

Luke portrays Peter in the act of proclaiming the resurrection as Jesus' coronation as gracious Sovereign over all people, including Gentiles (Acts 10). Paul tells how the resurrection of Jesus entails the future resurrection of all believers, because Jesus' resurrection means victory over all God's enemies, including death (1 Corinthians 15). John wants to provoke readers to deeper faith in the resurrected Jesus, for such faith means attachment to the invincible power of suffering love (John 20).

FIRST LESSON: ACTS 10:34–43

Peter's sermon at the house of Cornelius in Caesarea Maritima, the Roman capital of the province of Judea, is an important piece in Luke's presentation of Peter (Acts 9:32—12:23). Peter is about to fulfill his vocation as "fisher of human beings" (Luke 5:1–11).

The ministry of Jesus was confined to Israel, but the ministry of the new community will extend "to the ends of the earth," and that means the inclusion of Gentiles along with Jews and Samaritans (Acts 1:8). Greek-speaking Jewish Christians like Stephen have been portrayed as less than enthusiastic about the Jewish law and Jewish temple (Acts 6—7). So far Samaritans have been included (8:4–24), an Ethiopian eunuch has been baptized (8:26–40), and Saul/Paul, future apostle to the Gentiles, has been converted (9:1–20). However, the community has not taken the decisive move into the gentile world, even though everything has been heading in that direction. It is Peter, propelled by the Spirit, who will open a new phase in the history of God's people.

Peter begins his sermon in the house of Cornelius with the words, "Surely God shows no partiality" (v. 34). God is no taker of bribes, no respecter of persons, no tribal totem. Whatever people may do, and everyone knows how partial, biased, egocentric, and ethnocentric people are, "God shows no partiality."

On the contrary, the call goes out from God to people "in every nation" to come and enter the kingdom and enjoy the blessings of membership in the universal people of God. When Peter says that "any one who fears him and does what is right is acceptable to him" (v. 34), it sounds like a sermon on gaining God's favor by our own attitude and deeds. But Luke has quite eloquently undercut such a position in the parables of the lost coin, the lost sheep, and the two sons (Luke 15), in the story of the Pharisee and the tax collector (Luke 18:9–14), in the narrative about Zacchaeus (Luke 19:1–10), and in the word to one of the criminals crucified with Jesus (Luke 23:43). Each of these celebrates God's free and uncalculating grace. Such passages need to be kept in mind as we try to understand who is acceptable to God and on what grounds that acceptance is based.

Luke knows that some outsiders accuse the church with its message of grace of undermining morality, and he wishes to defend the church's proclamation and practice. His efforts are certainly not as sophisticated as Paul's, but that is what he is up to here. God is expansive and without partiality, he says, and, furthermore, good and God-fearing people can be found also outside Judaism. Luke is defending (perhaps a bit clumsily) gracious outreach and not what is sometimes called "works-righteousness." Whatever importance we humans may assign to blood and soil, class and status, ancestry and nation, Luke asserts that all these are nothing before God.

Peter's sermon is a thesaurus of Lukan ideas. God has shared a "word" (6:7) with Israel, "preaching good news" with the specific content of "peace" or wholeness (Luke 2:14; Acts 3:16) offered through Jesus Christ who is "Lord of all" (Acts 2:34–36). Everything started when at the Jordan "God anointed Jesus," spilling out on him "the Holy Spirit and power" (Acts 1:8). Jesus displayed his peculiar power by "doing good and healing all that were oppressed by the devil" (cf. Luke 22:25; Acts 2:22). In spite of all his benefactions and not because of any wrongdoing, he was put to death by human enemies (the cruel tree of the cross is their deed, 5:30), but he was raised by God (triumph over the grave is God's deed).

God raised him and "made him manifest" (v. 40; cf. 1:3) to chosen witnesses who ate and drank in his peaceable presence after his mighty resurrection (Luke 24:28–35, 41–43; Acts 1:4). Eating together means mutual acceptance in full fellowship, and so the resurrection appearances were acts of forgiveness and not merely proofs of livcliness.

The appearances meant commissioning. At the command of Jesus his witnesses have gone forth as heralds to proclaim his enthronement and to call people everywhere to bow the neck to him (Acts 1:8). He would embrace within his rule all religions and cultures and powers. He is the one "ordained by God to be judge of the living and the dead" (v. 42), the standard for assessing and valuing lives in the present and on the last day (Luke 17:30–31; 24:24–25).

"All the prophets" (v. 43) point to Jesus and the resurrection. God's kingdom has been inaugurated now that Jesus has been exalted, and the king wishes to celebrate his enthronement by distributing the gift of the Spirit and by declaring universal amnesty ("forgiveness of sins," v. 43).

His is a sovereignty different from Caesar's, not simply greater in power but differently powerful, delivering what Caesar only dimly conveys, genuine peace and freedom from the worst and most terrible oppressors, including even the demons. And the weapons of Jesus are not those of Caesar: not sword, not troops, not terror (cf. Luke 22:24–27). Luke envisions a great alternative to Caesar's empire, a new human community under the lordship of Jesus, and he holds that alternative vision before the eyes of his readers. Luke calls his readers to celebrate Christ's lordship by sharing his vision of a peaceable kingdom. That is a countercultural vision, and embracing it may mean mounting resistance to the status quo. Easter entices us to hope and to work for something greater than traditional personal, social, and political arrangements.

SECOND LESSON: 1 CORINTHIANS 15:19–26

Paul speaks of new horizons opened for the faithful by Christ, new horizons not limited to the days of this life. In earlier chapters of 1 Corinthians Paul has written about new forms of liveliness before death. He has dealt with perennial issues of human nature and Christian community: cliques, boasting, incest, lawsuits, fornication, asceticism, abstinence, marriage, divorce, idolatry, selfishness, ritualism, spirituality. Paul has summoned the Corinthians to practice now in this world the new life of love.

But in chapter 15 Paul deliberately turns from the here and now to that future when bodies are laid into cold tombs. Does Paul have a word about death, that most devastating of all limits, that toughest of all boundaries?

In 1 Cor. 15:12 Paul indicates that some Corinthian Christians were skeptical about the future resurrection of Christians. The exact basis of their denial remains a matter of dispute. Possibly they believed only in the immortality of the soul and not the continued existence of the material element; or they affirmed a future life only for those living at the time of Jesus' return (1 Thess. 4:15); or they spiritualized the resurrection tradition by teaching a present rebirth in baptism as the only necessary and possible renewal (cf. 2 Tim. 2:18; John 3:5; 5:24).

Does the Christian Gospel refer only to forms of newness on this side of death? Is the resurrection of Jesus a mere metaphor for fresh possibilities of life on earth? Are we confined (some would say "condemned") to proclaiming the new in terms of psychology and sociology? If so, resurrection means a new being, a new outlook, fresh hopefulness and optimism. Or resurrection means the possibility of a new social order, a new politics, a new economics. And so we translate the Pauline gospel into a call for fresh self-acceptance or a fresh campaign of civil disobedience, and point to that acceptance and that campaign as our celebration of Easter.

These may all have an honored part in our celebration, but are they the whole of it?

In 1 Corinthians 15 Paul looks hard at bodies rotting in the ground, and speaks of newness beyond the grave. Death has lost its status as international and universal boundary because Christ has been raised from the dead. The border is broken because Christ is not a mere private citizen. He is the first fruits (v. 20). His existence has cosmic import, and in that sense the only comparable existence is Adam's. Both Adam and Christ are universal progenitors, deep wellsprings— one of death and destruction, the other of life and praise of the Creator (vv. 21–22).

Paul speaks of two sovereignties: that of "God the Father" and that of "every rule and every authority and power" (v. 24) who are in fact the "enemies" of God (v. 25). Right now the latter continue their age-old reign, although their rule is under hard siege and has the word "finished" written all over it. Christ ("the Son") has set up an alternative kingdom, final and enduring.

Paul does not say that Christ reigns in heaven while the enemies reign on earth. He does not promise that the faithful departed go winging off to another world, where God holds undisputed sway. He is very far from saying that God is interested in souls while regarding bodies with an attitude of indifference. He says that Christ has been raised body and soul from death's grip and is working here and now to put all enemies under his feet (v. 25). Ancient rulers sometimes had their footstools inscribed with images of their enemies and literally rested their feet on those carved replicas. Christ will finally destroy all the enemies of God, including "the last enemy" (death, v. 26), and will rest the soles of his feet upon their necks. Then Christ will deliver sovereignty into the hands of God the Father. Then at last all things will be subject to God, and God will be "everything to everyone" (v. 28).

Paul insists that those who are already in Christ will not experience the full power of Christ's resurrection until his future appearance as Lord of all. Only later, at his powerful appearing, will the end *(to telos)* come.

Things must happen in a certain order, and we must recognize where we ourselves live on this chronology, says Paul. He says so because many Corinthians believed that the kingdom had already arrived and pointed to their spiritual gifts as evidence. Paul, by contradicting the Corinthians and speaking of the victory of God as still in the future, is not merely engaging in a war of words. He is turning the Corinthians to the work that still remains to be done in the present. That "work of the Lord" (v. 58) is described everywhere in 1 Corinthians as living in love *(agape)*, but nowhere more memorably than in chapter 13. Love is the true praise of God, and love builds true human community (14:4).

As Paul speaks of the future and insists on a future beyond death, he is anything but escapist. His teaching about the end and about things beyond the end supports his practical orientation to the needs of the Christian community now. It is easy for Christian communities to become so fascinated by his images and so wrapped up in them that they miss the solid connection Paul forges between the resurrection in the future and the call to love the sisters and brothers right now.

Paul places high value on the body and on the deeds done to one another in community through bodies. Furthermore, worship of God is not merely a matter of inward or spiritual acts. It involves the totality of our individual and social lives. Paul proclaims the resurrection of the body because he believes that God is on the way to renewing the whole complex reality that we call creation.

GOSPEL: JOHN 20:1–18

Beginning in John 13, the evangelist has spoken of "the Beloved Disciple." This mysterious figure, representing either the founder of the Johannine community or John's notion of the ideal disciple, does not appear at all in the other Gospels. However, the Fourth Evangelist found room for him at Jesus' last supper (13:23–25), at the trial (18:15–16), at the cross (19:25–27), and also at the tomb (20:2–10; cf. 21:7, 20–24).

In telling the Easter narrative, the evangelist grants to Mary Magdalene, Peter, and Thomas their own special forms of priority. They were first at the tomb, first to see Jesus, first to touch the resurrected Lord. But the Beloved Disciple has a surpassing priority all his own.

All of John 20 is a meditation on faith, and every man and woman named in the chapter comes to faith one way or another. The Beloved Disciple is praised as the first to believe, and he comes to faith in exemplary fashion. His Easter experience is held before readers' eyes as a lesson in crossing from nonfaith to faith, and that always means moving from death to life.

The earliest Christian tradition had described Peter as the first of the Twelve to see the resurrected Jesus; and Mary Magdalene was among the first women to see Jesus, hear his voice, and fall at his feet. The Fourth Gospel does not flatly contradict the tradition. It does not say that the Beloved Disciple was first to see, touch, or talk with the resurrected Jesus. The priority of the Beloved Disciple is of an altogether different sort. It has a different content.

The evangelist has carefully arranged the opening of the chapter (20:1–18) in order to highlight the priority of the Beloved Disciple. He begins with Mary Magdalene (20:1–2), interrupts her story to focus on the Beloved Disciple and Peter (20:3–10), and then returns to complete the narrative regarding Mary (20:11–18). By so structuring the material, the author has kept Mary's encounter with Jesus from overshadowing the faith of the Beloved Disciple.

Furthermore, the author's presentation of Mary and Peter (like his description of Thomas) reveals flaws in their attitudes. The evangelist portrays Mary's concern for the corpse of Jesus in a nearly comic light: "Where have you laid him? Tell me and I will come and single-handedly [!] carry him back to his tomb" (20:2, 13, 15). And note how Peter is treated. Peter and the Beloved Disciple race to the tomb together. The Beloved Disciple arrived first, but Peter entered the tomb first. Playing with notions of "first" and "second," the evangelist portrays Simon Peter as second to the Beloved Disciple in some respects although first in others. Both entered the tomb, but only of the Beloved Disciple is it said that he came to faith (v. 8).

The Beloved Disciple was the first to come to faith. That is his great priority. And he came to faith in illuminating fashion. Others need to see Jesus, or hear or touch him. The Beloved Disciple looked into the tomb and saw only the linen cloths left behind by Jesus (cf. the cloths binding Lazarus, 11:44). And that was enough. The Beloved Disciple looked at those graveclothes and read them like the pages of a book. What did the Beloved Disciple really "see" in those graveclothes so neatly laid aside in Jesus' tomb? He saw that Jesus used those wrappings and then discarded them forever. In doing the work of God, Jesus did not bypass death. He needed those cloths and that grave to fulfill his mission. By his death he has loved his own people all the way to the end (13:1). By his dying he conquered death. And so his dying has now become the source of real life.

Not until that moment at the tomb did the Beloved Disciple or any other follower of Jesus understand the scriptural promise of the victory of God (20:9). Victory comes not through acts of power or mere words of revelation but through the crucifixion, death, and burial of Jesus (cf. 12:24). The Beloved Disciple knew the Scriptures when he "saw" that life emerges from the death of God's Son.

The Beloved Disciple came to faith, and without further ado Mary Magdalene is reintroduced (v. 11). She learns nothing from Peter or the Beloved Disciple, but John wants readers to learn from her. She also bends over and looks into the tomb (cf. v. 5). She however sees not graveclothes but two angels in white seated on the shelf along the wall of the cave-tomb. One sat at the head, the other at the foot, as if posed to bring to mind the ark of the covenant in the Holy of Holies. The scene shouts that the crucified and resurrected Jesus is the place of most intimate meeting with God. He is the place of holy and creative communication between earth and heaven (cf. 1:51; 2:21).

Mary does not yet understand, although readers should. She straightens and turns, as though empty tomb and angels have made no impression. She sees Jesus without recognizing him (v. 14). He asks a twofold question, "Why are you weeping?" and "Whom are you seeking?" The latter question echoes Jesus' first words in the Gospel (1:38). And they confront readers with the same question, What and whom are you seeking? What is the goal of all your living and striving?

Mary stands weeping, displaying an impressive devotion to the dead Jesus. She wants his corpse (v. 15). That is not Christian faith. She is drawn closer to faith as Jesus speaks her name, "Mary!" (cf.

10:3) She grasps him (cf. Matt. 28:9) but Jesus still rebukes her, saying, "Cease touching me." He has not yet "ascended to the Father" (cf. 3:13; 6:62). Mary is here pictured as thinking that the goal of her relationship with Jesus is achieved in meeting and touching Jesus outside the tomb. But the evangelist rejects that notion as surely as he rejects Mary's questing after the corpse of Jesus.

Fellowship between Jesus and Mary has not yet reached its goal in their encounter outside the tomb. Jesus' words to Mary recall all he has said previously in the Farewell Discourse (chaps. 13—17) and elsewhere about his ascent to the Father and about drawing all people to himself (cf. 12:32).

Through all his life and then especially through the cross, Jesus progresses upward to that same oneness with the Father that he had enjoyed before his descent (1:1). Then after the cross and Easter, the Father and the Son come and make their home with the disciples (14:23, Sixth Sunday of Easter). "I in them and thou in me" is the way Jesus expresses the goal (17:23, Seventh Sunday of Easter). Mary must cease clinging to Jesus' feet. She must relinquish the old physical and social contact and exchange it for the new spiritual relationship described as a mutual indwelling. That new relationship is available to women and men of every generation and place. Indeed, celebrating Easter means entering more fully into God—and inviting God to enter more fully into us.

How can that happen? John points neither to sight and touch nor to shattering miracles and proofs. A recent book by Albert Hebert, *Raised from the Dead* (Tan Books, 1986), narrates "true stories of 400 resurrection miracles," including resurrections of people buried for several years and raisings of people whose bodies were mutilated or reduced to skeletons by decay. These stories are certainly "amazing," as the book jacket asserts. But even in such quantity these stories of resurrections seem insufficient to generate Easter faith. John is right. Jesus spoke a benediction on those "who have not seen and yet believe" (20:29). And John declares that he has written his whole story of Jesus to engender Easter faith (20:30–31, Second Sunday of Easter). These pages of his on the vulnerability and love of Jesus are the graveclothes that alone can initiate us into faith. They are enough.

Easter Evening or Easter Monday

Lutheran	Roman Catholic	Episcopal	Common Lectionary
Dan. 12:1c–3 or Jon. 2:2–9	Acts 2:14, 22–32	Acts 5:29a, 30–32 or Dan. 12:1–3	Acts 5:29–32 or Dan. 12:1–3
1 Cor. 5:6–8		1 Cor. 5:6b–8 or Acts 5:29a, 30–32	1 Cor. 5:6–8 or Acts 5:29–32
Luke 24:13–49	Matt. 28:8–15	Luke 24:13–35	Luke 24:13–49

Daniel and Paul see an intimate connection between resurrection and morality. Resurrection is God's act and God's verdict, confirming the life of the righteous ones (Daniel). Easter answers the cry that justice might at long last roll down like many waters. Paul declares that Jesus' resurrection implies a new way of life, free of the leaven of immorality. Easter echoes and brings to fulfillment themes of Passover and dreams of liberation. Easter does not mean escapism but signifies the renewal of ethics.

FIRST LESSON: DANIEL 12:1–3

The Book of Daniel was written at a time (ca. 165 B.C.) when Antiochus Epiphanes was pressuring pious Israelites to give up loyalty to the law and adopt Hellenistic ways. Antiochus, the "little horn" (Dan. 7:8), installed an altar to Zeus (the desolating sacrilege) in the temple at Jerusalem and summoned Jews to sacrifice to his god (11:31). When persuasion failed, he did not shrink from torture and brutal persecution.

Visions conclude the Book of Daniel. They are uttered by "one in the likeness of the sons of men," that is, by a humanlike figure, in contrast to the vision of beasts representing cruel and godless nations. That great human figure offers teaching in praise of the practical wisdom called "righteousness."

The visions promise that Michael, "the great prince who has charge of your people," will arise at the end during a time of great trouble that will threaten the very life of the nation. Michael will deliver all those whose names are written in the Book of Life (cf. Exod. 32:32–33; Ps. 69:28; Rev. 3:5). Sleepers (1 Thess. 4:13; Matt. 27:52) in the tombs will arise, some to "everlasting life," some to face an awful sentence of condemnation.

In many ways these visions form an appropriate conclusion. "Daniel" means "My judge is God." God is the only One whose judgment finally counts, and the Book of Daniel encourages readers to place every other judge and judgment under God's judgment. The book does not even summon Israelites to trust in the Maccabean guerrilla movement. At most, those warrior-Israelites will be "a little help" (11:34). God will be the help of those who wait patiently. And God will reward "wise ones," teachers who encouraged them with instruction in wisdom. The wisdom exalted in this book is the practical wisdom of obedience to God's will.

In 12:1–3 we have a poem praising the pious and the wise. These wise are like Daniel. They practice and teach righteousness and so turn many to righteousness. And theirs is an especially great reward. They will shine like the stars forever, a startling image picked up in the speech of Jesus at Matt. 13:43.

This one lesson, Dan. 12:1–3, is the only Old Testament Scripture to be read in church during the Easter season of Year C. The ancient Hebrew Bible actually has few passages that speak directly of individual bodily resurrection. And so the Book of Acts regularly supplies the first lesson in all three years for the Sundays between Easter and Pentecost.

SECOND LESSON: 1 CORINTHIANS 5:6–8

Paul is apparently writing the Corinthians in the spring of the year at Passover time (cf. 1 Cor. 16:8). He has Passover imagery on his mind and he knows it may be on theirs also. Yet the celebration of the Christian Passover, of Good Friday–Easter, is not seasonal, not a matter of one day or even of three, but is synonymous with Christian existence in general. Jews rid their homes of leaven in preparation for Passover, and Paul summons Christians to rid their lives of everything unholy, unclean, and polluting, since "Christ our Passover has been sacrificed for us."

There is nothing exceptional in that declaration. Controversy begins when people are asked to define what is holy and what is unholy. Precisely what needs to be thrown out? Paul and the Corinthians had different ideas. They were "puffed up" (5:2; RSV has "arrogant"), a marvelous phrase in Greek, suggesting dough puffed up by yeast or leaven. And the Corinthians had not wanted to throw out the incestuous member. They had turned him into a hero and even admired how "liberated" he was. The way to celebrate our Passover, says Paul, is to get rid of him and all yeast like him.

In this lesson Paul describes the church as "the bread of God." In fact, Paul wants the congregation to be not just any bread, but unleavened bread, free of contaminating yeast. When the church really is "God's bread," then it will not be riddled with factions. Nor will it humiliate the poor. But it will be filled with omnipotent love, just as Christ is bread broken for us (1 Cor. 11:17–32). When the church is such bread, then the world will see something of the mind of God (cf. Luke 24:13–35, a portion of the Gospel for this day).

GOSPEL: LUKE 24:13–49

Everything in Luke 24 fits into a single day (24:1, 13, 33) and all the events are played out in a single locale: Jerusalem and its immediate vicinity.

Luke's theme in the first part of the lection (24:13–35) is not simply the movement of two disciples toward Emmaus. His real theme is his readers' own journeys. Readers are invited to progress with the disciples from initial distress and unbelief (vv. 4, 5, 11, 17, 25, 37) to final faith and joy (vv. 41, 45, 52–53). And once those movements have taken place, disciples can move out from concerns of self and begin to embrace others with the love of the resurrected Christ (24:47–49).

The Emmaus story is traditionally interpreted as dealing with the presence of Christ, first of all in the reading of Scripture (vv. 13–27) and then in the Eucharist (vv. 28–35). But there is more to the passage.

The two Emmaus disciples walk dejectedly away from the holy city. They are sheep scattering. Jesus joins them, but they are unable to recognize him (vv. 15–16). What will it take to open the eyes of these two disciples? Or the eyes of readers?

Luke frequently comments on the lack of understanding among Jesus' disciples. Why do the inhabitants of the holy city fail to understand the conditions of peace (19:42)? Why do pious people not grasp the meaning of Scripture (Acts 13:27)? How can the suffering of Jesus be a vital part of God's plans for the world (Luke 9:44–45; 18:31–34)?

Jesus asks what they are talking about as they walk from Jerusalem. With their eyes still kept from knowing him (24:16), they begin to share their frustrations, detailing their hope of redemption in moving terms. They speak of Jesus as "a prophet mighty in deed and word before God and all the people" (v. 19). But they imagine that Jesus' death has defeated God's plan. They view his death as an unjust act of rebellious humanity, perpetrated by "our chief priests and rulers" (v. 20). They need to see it as an integral part of God's plan, as a deed that God puts to good use in heading toward good ends. What they require is not just the knowledge that Jesus is alive. They need to know the mystery of God's design for the cosmos.

The Emmaus disciples continue by speaking to Jesus of the events of early Easter morning, of how women failed to find the corpse but had "a vision of angels" who trumpeted the news that Jesus lives (vv. 22–24). But, they say, the report of the women failed to persuade any of the other disciples (vv. 11, 24). Even at this point Jesus does not simply reveal himself as living but instead begins to offer them teaching.

Jesus begins to instruct them and the readers in God's plan. It is not easy for them or for us to grasp it. On the one hand, it is simply a fact that God's prophets and envoys, arriving with God's word in their mouths, are rejected generation after generation, even by God's people. Martyrdom is part of the cost of being a prophet. In fact, death is often a sign that prophets have successfully fulfilled their responsibility to God in spite of the resistance of humankind. The prophetic predecessors and the apostolic successors of Jesus will live and die by the same pattern.

Furthermore, if the followers of Jesus are to understand the mind of God, they must recognize that God does not use the same tactics as Roman emperors. God is not a despot like the one ruling Rome, and God's power is different from human power. The kingdom of God is not just like the Roman kingdom only bigger and mightier. Its might is of a different order altogether. God rules by the power of suffering love.

So Jesus speaks to the Emmaus disciples about how it was "necessary" (v. 26) for the Christ to suffer. The suffering of the Christ means that God refuses to resort to power in inaugurating the kingdom of God. The cross speaks of the ingathering of the lost and the creation of new community by means of forgiveness and suffering love (cf. 23:34).

They arrived at the village of Emmaus, and Jesus entered their house. He sat with them at their table but he himself acted as host. He took the bread, blessed and broke it, and shared it with them (v. 30). At that moment scales fell from their eyes and their understandings, and they knew him (v. 31).

Did they simply recognize who the stranger was? Or was their new knowledge deeper? Surely it was connected with the words Jesus had spoken on the way. And surely readers are meant to see here the climax of the many meals Jesus shares with others in the Gospel of Luke. He ate at the home of a Pharisee and accepted the devotion of a sinful woman (Luke 7:36–50). He fed great hungry crowds after teaching them about the kingdom of God and healing all their sick (9:10–17). He welcomed tax collectors and sinners and broke bread with them (15:1–2). The inner circle of disciples misunderstood him and would betray and deny him, yet he sat at table with them (22:14).

In the breaking of bread at Emmaus, the disciples see that their companion is Jesus, but they see more. They finally begin to see that Jesus suffered on the cross because he is the Christ of a kingdom of peace founded not by military conquest with weapons of iron but built on the vulnerability of forgiving grace.

Bread broken and consumed conjures up all the familiar images of Jesus in his loving and self-giving contact with the ill, the poor, the outcast. Diverse human beings with all their imperfections sharing a meal with one another is Luke's most powerful symbol of the kingdom of God. In that meal shared with Jesus at Emmaus, the disciples began to understand God's project. "Their eyes were opened in the breaking of the bread" (v. 31).

Back in Jerusalem, Jesus appeared to all the assembled disciples and shared a meal with them (vv. 33–43). So all were initiated into a new understanding, as the Emmaus disciples had been (vv. 44–45). Then they are ready to be commissioned as envoys of the kingdom of peace. They are to call "all nations" to surrender to God in repentance and to receive from God forgiveness and the embrace of love. The equipment they require for their calling is not described as a course in social planning. Certainly it is not command of legions or lessons in military strategy. It is the Holy Spirit, described here as "the promise of my Father" and "power from on high." Verses 44–49 appear again, together with 24:50–53, as the first part of the lection for the Ascension of Our Lord.

The Second Sunday of Easter

Lutheran	Roman Catholic	Episcopal	Common Lectionary
Acts 5:12, 17–32	Acts 5:12–16	Acts 5:12a, 17–22, 25–29 or Job 42:1–6	Acts 5:27–32
Rev. 1:4–18	Rev. 1:9–11, 12–13, 17–19	Rev. 1:(1–8) 9–19 or Acts 5:12a, 17–22, 25–29	Rev. 1:4–8
John 20:19–31	John 20:19–31	John 20:19–31	John 20:19–31

Jesus' new life is not for Jesus alone. Easter announces that Jesus has been raised to new standing as Lord of the whole universe. He has been exalted by resurrection to the right hand of God (Acts 5). Although slain, he lives and now stands "between the throne and the four living creatures and among the elders" in the throne room of heaven (Revelation 5). Nails and spear thrust could not hold him, and he has emerged from the tomb as victor over death.

As Lord of the cosmos and conqueror of death, he is worthy of angelic adoration (Revelation 5) and human allegiance (John 20).

FIRST LESSON: ACTS 5:12, 17–32

Easter is just like God, for as Gabriel trumpets at the start of Luke-Acts, "With God nothing is impossible" (Luke 1:37). And Luke tells us what this means. For Jesus it means birth from God at life's start, rescue from angry crowds at the beginning of his public ministry (4:30), and rescue from Hades at the end (24:5). God's power breaks out in miracles of healing and exorcism and in raisings of the dead (Luke 7:11–17; 8:40–55; Acts 9:36–42; 20:7–12). And more. For disciples and all companions of Jesus, God's power means narrow escape: prison doors open, chains fall away, guards are stumped, stoning fails, shipwreck is not fatal, and poisonous snakes fall dead into the fire. God's power means finding the lost (Luke 2:41–52; 15:1–32; 19:1–10) and exalting the humble (Luke 1:46–55; 2:34; 13:30; 14:11; 15:24, 32; 18:14).

All these are connected to Easter. For Luke, every healing or rescue is a little resurrection, a piece of the same power that erupted in its purest form on Easter. The resurrection of Jesus is marvelous but it is not, at least not according to Luke, something strange or unique. It is rather the most stunning and electrifying example of how God is always acting to subdue the forces of chaos.

Luke wrote of the resurrection of Jesus partly to encourage perseverance and hope in the face of tribulation (Acts 14:22). God's own people—pious, faithful, and good—regularly fall victim to illness, misfortune, or persecution. Luke heartens them with the message that God will overrule their enemies. Perhaps God will engineer an escape in history, or it may be that God will rescue them on the other side of death. But God will never abandon these holy ones.

In Acts, Luke often specifies that the opponents of the Christians were not the Jews in general, not the crowds, and not the Pharisees, but the Sadducees (4:1–2; 5:17). Note the contrasts with "the people" in 5:26 and with the Pharisees in 26:6–10. Resistance is not confined to the Sadducees but because of their skepticism about the resurrection they are regularly pictured as the opposition, as they are here in Acts 5.

The high priestly party, the aristocratic families centered in Jerusalem, are the hub of the opposition. One of their number, "the captain of the temple" (4:1; 5:24), had the task of crowd control and other police functions in the temple.

The apostles had already been taken into custody once (4:3) and released with a stern warning to stop speaking about Jesus and the resurrection (4:2, 17–18). But here they were again, teaching and healing in Solomon's Portico (5:12), the long arcade traversing the entire eastern side of the temple platform. So once again the party of the Sadducees moved to stem the apostolic preaching and had the apostles thrown into jail (5:17–18).

But at night "an angel of the Lord" opened the prison doors and led them out of prison so that they could "speak to the people all the words of this Life" (v. 20). Throughout Acts, God liberates and empowers the apostles through angel or Spirit (and of course the Sadducees believe in neither, 23:8) for one purpose only: bold proclamation.

The officers report a resurrection-like wonder: "We found the prison securely locked and the sentries standing at the doors, but when we opened it we found no one inside" (v. 23). This sounds like the discovery of Jesus' empty tomb. Once again the apostles were taken into custody, gently and quietly, for the police feared being "stoned by the people" (v. 26).

The high priest as chair of the Sanhedrin criticized the apostles for ignoring the official warning "not to teach in this name." What they had been teaching in the name of Jesus was life and salvation and resurrection (3:15–16; 4:2, 12; 5:20). Ironically, what the Sadducees feared was their own death at the hands of crowds whipped up to vengeful passion by the preaching of the apostles (5:26, 28).

Even more emphatically than at 4:19, the apostles here (5:29) utter a response like that of Shadrach, Meshach, and Abednego when the king had demanded their obeisance (Dan. 3:18). Greek audiences would hear an echo of Socrates' rejoinder to his accusers, "I obey god rather than you" (Plato, *Apology* 29D). The apostles had heard the voice of God speaking to them in the resurrection of Jesus from the dead. And they were obedient to that word.

The crucifixion and resurrection of Jesus are acts reflecting diametrically opposed estimates of Jesus. In the resurrection God has spoken an everlasting yes to Jesus. Hanging Jesus on a tree expressed not only the contempt of human leaders for Jesus but their conviction that Jesus was a thing impure and accursed (Deut. 21:23).

Resurrection not only restored Jesus to life but exalted Jesus to God's "right hand as Leader and Savior" (3:15; 7:35). Jesus is the ruler of the New Age, and it is his wish to distribute not feared sentences of death on his enemies (v. 28) but gifts of amnesty ("forgiveness of sins") to a humble and penitent people.

The task of those who follow Jesus Christ is to bear witness to the unique sovereignty of Jesus. That involves uttering bold critiques of other rules and rulers. And the Holy Spirit is the power of God equipping disciples for that task.

Each of the sermons in the first half of Acts stresses some particular piece of the Christian message as Luke understands it. In 5:28–32 Luke focuses on celebrating Easter by being in step with God. That may very well mean being out of step with some sacred cows, some respected authorities, some revered ideas. When people begin to trust the sovereignty of God in Jesus Christ, not only do scales of unbelief fall away, but the powers of the world begin to be unmasked. The arrogance and dangers lurking in the claims of political powers, for example, begin to be revealed.

SECOND LESSON: REVELATION 1:4–8

Luke and John could hardly be farther apart in terms of attitudes toward government. Luke always seems to be such a positive thinker, able to see the bright side of things, even of Caesar's government. In Acts, Luke pictures Paul as cheerfully and optimistically appealing his case to Rome, apparently imagining that Paul will get a fair hearing before the tyrant Nero. On the other hand, John the Divine Theologian is the great naysayer. And yet Acts 5:29 and Rev. 1:4–8 seem to have much in common.

Individual congregations will be named in Revelation 2 and 3, but the Revelation as a whole is addressed to "the seven churches that are in [the province of] Asia." That seems to mean that the seven individually named congregations are a kind of paradigm of the church as a whole.

And it is not only John who addresses the church but also God, and the Spirit, and Jesus Christ. God is the one "who is and who was and who is to come" (cf. Exod. 3:14), the one who holds all times in divine hands. The "seven spirits before God's throne" is a surprising description of the one Holy Spirit but understandable as a graphic way to speak of the full and overflowing energy of God ceaselessly pouring forth spiritual gifts into the life of the cosmos.

And Jesus is "the ruler *(ho archōn)* of kings on earth" (Rev. 1:5; Ps. 89:27), in spite of the fact that as "the faithful witness" *(ho martys ho pistos;* cf. 1 Tim. 6:13) he shed his blood, pierced through by agents of those same kings. He was witness against the kings on earth, stubbornly opposed to them and their rule and their spirit, and he let them know it.

His blood is not a sign of defeat but of victory, for by it the church has been loved to the utmost, washed from sins, and liberated. As priest, the king offered up his life. In the process he made his people both kingly and priestly, both "a royal household," the children of the great king, and also a body of priests, a community dedicated to the perpetual practice of holy service to God (cf. Exod. 19:6).

Put to death, he is yet "first born of the dead," the first and by no means the last to rise from a martyr's grave. And he is "coming with the clouds" to exercise universal dominion after universal judgment. At that judgment the tables will be turned. A Roman judge once held him prisoner, heard his case, found him wanting, and had him taken away to be pierced in hand, foot, and side. That pierced one comes as final judge to settle all accounts.

Easter faith means trusting that the one with whom we have to do, the faithful and just judge under whose keen eye we live, is not Caesar or some agent of Caesar but the Lord God, the Omnipotent, who is and who was and who is to come. The coming one is mighty in judgment, but even more awesome in love. The coming Judge is the one who gave his life for the life of humankind. The coming Judge is the gracious Savior of all.

GOSPEL: JOHN 20:19–31

John here continues his meditation on the theme of faith, begun in the first half of chapter 20 (Gospel for Easter Sunday). This lection has three parts: "Peace to You" (20:19–23), "Unless I See" (20:24–29), and "Life in His Name" (20:30–31).

The disciples, locked in fear and unbelief, were for the moment "lost" in John's technical sense of that word (see John 17, Seventh Sunday of Easter). They were not in fellowship with Jesus but were overcome by the power of the world, separated from Jesus and the Father (cf. 16:32). Yet Jesus does not leave them "orphans" or "desolate" (14:18) but comes to them, calling and gathering them to himself, granting peace (14:27; 16:33).

"Peace" *(shalom)* was and still is the common Hebrew word for ordinary greetings. But the word is used also at significant moments of revelation (Judges 6:23; Dan. 10:19). With his peace Jesus penetrates the solid wall of the disciples' fear and unbelief.

Jesus displays his hands and side, not as in Luke 24:36–43 to prove his solidity and corporeality, nor merely to establish his identity. He does it to exhibit the wounds by which he has overcome the world (John 19:36–37; Zech. 12:10). The wounds of Jesus have the power to remove fear and fill with joy.

Perhaps John notes that the door of the room was bolted, in order to guard against materialistic ideas of the body of the resurrected Jesus. It is easy to leap to false conclusions in this narrative in which Jesus offers his body to be touched. The author is not trying to define the resurrected body of Jesus as solid or as ghostly. He wants to focus on the mystery of Jesus' presence in the postcrucifixion world and on the presence of the wounds in Jesus' hands and side—there even after resurrection.

Jesus gave them peace and breathed out the Spirit upon them (cf. 1:33), as God breathed life into Adam (Gen. 2:7; Wisd. 15:11) and poured out life on the dry bones filling the valley (Ezek. 37:9). The crucified and resurrected Jesus is the agent of the new creation, the new Genesis.

When women and men are "one" with God in Christ, united by a single indestructible stream of life, then they are ready to be sent as Jesus was himself sent (17:18, 21, 23). They are commissioned for a ministry of the forgiveness of sins. In the Fourth Gospel the one great sin is unbelief. Followers of Jesus have the one great task of destroying sin by calling people to repentance and bringing them to faith.

The disciples immediately have the opportunity to begin their new vocations as missionaries. They go and proclaim to Thomas the Easter message: "We have seen the Lord." That is, the crucified Jesus has overcome the world and is victorious forever. At that moment Thomas had the opportunity to be the first person in the history of the world to come to faith on the basis of a word on the lips of Christian missionaries. In previous appearances (John 11:16; 14:5) Thomas has been pictured as one who fails to understand the path Jesus travels to the cross. For him the way of the cross is the way of destruction.

Here, instead of coming to faith, Thomas demands a specific piece of evidence (cf. 4:48). He wants not simply to handle the body of Jesus but to see and touch the mark of the nails and spear in his hands and side. He does not want to know whether the resurrected one is solid. He doubts whether the glorified one can really be identical with the crucified one. What can the cross have to do with God's power and glory?

The following Sunday Jesus comes to Thomas without scolding and meets his demands point for point. "Put your finger here and see my hands . . . my side." Mortal wounds really do belong to the eternal Son of God. And those wounds are not simply part of Jesus' past. They belong to him forever. Those scars will never fade. They proclaim his boundless love for his own (13:1). Because they declare his obedience to the Father and his scorn for the evil one, they are his marks of victory forever.

The doubter turns confessor at the sight of those wounds in the body of the resurrected one: "My Lord and my God." The crucified Jesus is "Lord and God." He is God in his turning to the world. He is in the Father and the Father is in him (10:38). Whoever has seen and heard the Son who went in love to the cross, has seen and heard the Father (14:9; cf. Mark 15:39).

Jesus then pronounces a benediction not upon Thomas alone but upon all those who believe without benefit of the signs and sights demanded by Thomas. Blessed are all those who come to faith without laying eyes or hands on Jesus. Blessed are those who come to faith simply on the basis of the story concerning Jesus. Blessed are believers of the second, third, and all subsequent generations.

The topic of John 20 has been Christian faith—its beginning, its end, its content. Now at the close of the chapter (20:30–31), the author announces that he is aware that Jesus performed far more signs than those recorded in this book. Yet his selection suffices. In fact this book will serve as a substitute for physical contact with Jesus in generation after generation (cf. John 20:1–18, Easter Sunday). The words of John's book have power to generate and then deepen faith in Jesus as Christ and Son of God and so bestow life. Faithful reception of the testimony of this book will bring forgiveness, the destruction of sin, movement from darkness to light, from hostility to friendship with God.

The Third Sunday of Easter

Lutheran	Roman Catholic	Episcopal	Common Lectionary
Acts 9:1–20	Acts 5:27b–32, 40b–41	Acts 9:1–19a or Jer. 32:36–41	Acts 9:1–20
Rev. 5:11–14	Rev. 5:11–14	Rev. 5:6–14 or Acts 9:1–19a	Rev. 5:11–14
John 21:1–14	John 21:1–19 or John 21:1–14	John 21:1–14	John 21:1–19 or John 21:15–19

The lessons last week insisted on Jesus' Lordship and celebrated it in a hymn of angels, a confession to Jesus, and testimony before the Sanhedrin. This week the lessons are full of talk about persecution.

According to Luke (Acts 9), Paul, snorting with hatred, heads toward Damascus to take Christ's confessors captive and is himself taken captive by the Lord. John, banished to the island of Patmos as a prisoner of the state, smoulders with resentment against Rome's haughty power, and he pours out his vision of the sovereignty of the Lamb (Revelation 5). On the shores of the Sea of Galilee, Jesus commissions Peter for his ministry and simultaneously prophesies his martyrdom (John 21).

All three lessons stand in terrible agreement. Even after Easter, after Jesus' elevation to the right hand of God, life is not easy for Lord or disciples. The universe has a new center, but for the time being the lordship of Jesus is not plainly visible for all to see. It can only be confessed in faith and commitment, often to the accompaniment of suffering.

FIRST LESSON: ACTS 9:1–20

Acts contains not just one but three separate accounts of the conversion of Paul (9:1–19; 22:4–16; 26:9–18; cf. Paul's own version in Gal. 1:13–14). "Saul" is the apostle's Jewish name, and "Paul" his Greek name. At Acts 13:9, as Paul and Barnabas leave the eastern Mediterranean and launch out on the first mission into predominantly

Greek-speaking territory, Luke switches from "Saul" to "Paul." It will be convenient already here to speak of the apostle as "Paul."

But should we speak of this turning point in Paul's life as a "conversion"? Often that word implies abandoning idolatry for the true religion or turning one's back on a life of moral turpitude to embrace sobriety, ethics, and lawfulness. That kind of a turning is not what the event before Damascus was about. Paul of course does emerge from the moment changed, with a new orientation and a new mission. He steps forth with fresh convictions about God and the people of God because of his encounter with the resurrected Jesus.

Before Damascus, Paul sided with all those who had killed Jesus and opposed the preaching and preachers of the young church (Acts 7:58—8:1). He was in fact on his way to Damascus to stamp out the church in that ancient city. Paul's mission was sanctioned by the high priest (Caiaphas was high priest till A.D. 36). So Luke pictures two movements issuing forth from Jerusalem: one made propaganda for Jesus, and the other carried a tough word against Jesus.

What is now called "Christianity" was then called "the Way" (19:9, 23; 22:4; 24:14, 22). For Luke, Christian life is a way to be followed or a path to be traveled behind Jesus. Jesus goes the way first as Pioneer and Pathfinder, leading perhaps through tribulation to the glory of life (3:15; 5:31).

As Paul and his companions neared Damascus, "a light from heaven" flashed about them. Paul fell to the ground and heard a voice repeating his Jewish name: "Saul, Saul!" Solemnity? Scolding? Shaming? Shepherd calling his sheep? (cf. Luke 6:46; 8:24; 10:41; 22:31; cf. Acts 26:14). And then a startling question, "Why are you persecuting me?" (v. 4).

Paul perhaps pictured his mission as a crusade to stop people from calling on the name of Jesus (4:2, 17; 5:28). But he had no idea he was persecuting Jesus himself. For Paul, Jesus was dead, and how could he imagine that he was persecuting a dead man? But the Lord Jesus identifies with his own and is personally insulted at the persecution of his own. His honor is at stake, and here he intervenes.

The revolutionary character of the event is underscored by Paul's three-day blindness and fasting (vv. 8–9). He had come toward Damascus full of the conceit that he was possessed of powerful vision. He was now plunged to the ground and into darkness, dependent on the guiding of others. For three days he was like a child in the womb, like Jonah in the fish, like Jesus in the grave: without light, waiting.

The magnitude of this call is further emphasized in the conversation between the Lord and Ananias, a pious (22:12) Christian disciple at Damascus. The Lord addressed him in a dream or vision (9:10–16), commissioning him to seek out Paul in the house of Judas on the street called Straight. Paul for his part has been led to expect someone who will lay healing hands on him. Ananias objects, pointing to Paul's reputation as a hater and persecutor of the church (vv. 13–14).

But the Lord recommends Paul to Ananias as "a chosen instrument of mine" (Jer. 50:25), chosen by God to "carry [God's] name" (3:16), that is, to proclaim the redemptive acts of God, to "the Gentiles and kings and sons of Israel." And in that work Paul will learn "how much he must suffer" in accord with the mysterious plan of God (14:22) "for the sake of the name" of God (4:12). Suffering and fidelity to God's commissioning go hand in hand everywhere in Luke-Acts (cf. Luke 24:13–35).

In pious obedience Ananias found Paul, laid accepting hands on him and called him "brother" (6:1; 22:13). He explained that he had come from the Lord that Paul might both regain his sight and be filled with the Holy Spirit (v. 17). Paul had gone forth from Jerusalem with the power to arrest and extradite (or to transport secretly across frontiers). He is now receiving a fresh and far different mission with the backing of the power of the Spirit of God (cf. 1:6–8). His progress will not be achieved by one powerful stroke delivered upon another but will be marked by suffering crowned with glory.

The man who had left Jerusalem thinking that he saw so clearly had been blind for three days. Now "something like scales" fell from his eyes and he could see again. He had been fasting and waiting in that three-day period, and now he rose up from blindness and fasting; he was baptized and fortified with food, sharing with new sisters and brothers in the new teaching and fellowship (2:41–42).

Paul traveled to Damascus with murder on his mind (9:1), and he returned as an envoy of the Author of life (3:15; 9:20–21). Paul's trademark after Damascus was the proclamation of the resurrected Jesus in the synagogues of the Jews and the marketplaces of the Greeks. He proclaimed "Jesus," the incarnate, vulnerable, crucified Jesus, as "the Son of God" (9:20), as Christ and Lord exalted to the right hand of God (2:22–36; 1 Cor. 1:22–24).

That Easter proclamation makes its way with difficulty in a world where it must compete with other "gospels." Celebrating Easter means saying yes to the lordship of Jesus, and it means speaking a simultaneous no to this world's "many gods and many lords" (1 Cor. 8:5–6). That is dangerous work. Before his call, Paul breathed out murder (9:1). Afterward, his enemies sought to murder him (9:29).

SECOND LESSON: REVELATION 5:11-14

An inaugural vision of one like a son of man (1:9–20) is followed by the seven letters to the seven churches (Revelation 2—3). Then John entered in ecstatic trance through an open door into heaven, described in terms of an imperial throne room (4:1–2). His eyes fasten first on the "one seated on the throne". And it most certainly is not the Roman caesar.

That great seated One holds in the right hand a scroll, full of writing, inscribed on both sides (5:1), and the call goes out, "Who is worthy to open the scroll?" Who can interpret the deep secrets of the universe? Who really knows the mind of God? At first no one is found worthy to open the scroll or to look into it, and the seer weeps much.

God's thoughts are higher than our thoughts. God's plans are shrouded in mystery, and especially in dark times God's management of the universe seems like no management at all. What is God up to? What, if anything, is guiding the course of history? Caesar and the politicians? Impersonal laws of nature? Economic forces? Is the world lacking in pattern or sense or goal?

Then one of the elders commanded the seer to cease weeping and to lift his eyes to "the Lion of the tribe of Judah" (cf. Gen. 49:9). The seer looks up expectantly, but he *sees* something different from what he has *heard,* or what he sees is a surprising fulfillment of what he has heard. Instead of a Lion he sees "a Lamb standing as though it had been slain," once slaughtered but now forever victorious. The Lamb approaches the throne and takes the scroll. Luke tells us how Jesus once stepped to the lectern in the synagogue of Nazareth, took the scroll, opened it, read from Isaiah, and then sat down to interpret the prophecy by pointing to his own presence (Luke 4:16–21). The other Gospels also portray Jesus as interpreter of Scripture and exegete of the mind of God (John 1:18).

By describing Jesus as "the Lamb who was slain," the seer portrays Jesus not as sage or prophet only. Jesus is the martyr of God who forever bears the marks of the world's misunderstanding and rejection. And yet he lives by the mighty approval of God which we call resurrection.

The Lamb takes the scroll, and immediately the four living creatures and the twenty-four elders fall down and sing a new song, praising the death of the Lamb as the powerful ransoming of humanity for God (5:3–10). That historic shedding of blood was Jesus' no to Caesar and to all the blandishments of this cosmos, and it was his resounding yes to God and to the will of God. And so his death is the basis of his worthiness celebrated in the new song.

Then the seer witnessed a great sight: the throne, the living creatures, and the elders were surrounded by a mighty chorus of angels, numbering "myriads of myriads and thousands of thousands." Together they break forth in a chant praising "the Lamb who was slain." The presence of the Lamb means that this vision differs decisively from other great visions of God enthroned in heaven (cf. 2 Kings 22:19–22; Isa. 6:1–7; Ezek. 1:4–28). Only the slain but victorious Lamb can interpret the mind and heart of God. The cross and resurrection are keys to unlocking the mysteries of God.

That great doxology of the angels (v. 12) is answered in antiphonal fashion by "every creature in heaven and on earth and under the earth and in the sea, and all therein." This must be a vision of the future, for in the present many creatures great and small still resist the truth displayed in the crucifixion and resurrection of Jesus. They ridicule it and reject it as they live life day by day.

Yet it is true and will be true. Whenever people raise songs of obedience and trust, the four living creatures shout approval with their "Amen" and the elders fall down and worship. Celebrating Easter does not mean adopting a naive stance of simple-minded blindness to the power of sin and ignorance in the world. It means rejoicing in God's self-revelation at cross and empty tomb. It means praising the God of omnipotent love with heart and life.

GOSPEL: JOHN 21:1–19

The final chapter in John's Gospel meditates once more on relations among Jesus and Peter and the Beloved Disciple. The chapter holds up to the reader familiar symbols of the church: catching fish, providing bread, feeding sheep, following the Lord, obeying his will, enduring martyrdom, bearing witness.

The scene is the Sea of Tiberias (= Sea of Galilee) where Jesus had fed the five thousand (6:1) and where he had revealed himself suddenly as the "I AM" (6:16–21). Seven disciples are present as witnesses, and five of them are named. Perhaps these seven are a symbol for the whole church (cf. Revelation 2—3). At any rate, the chapter wrestles with questions confronting the post-Easter community.

Peter had led the others in a night of fishing. Early in the morning Jesus stood unrecognized on the shore. At night without him they had caught nothing; in the morning, in his presence and at his command, they will be led to bounty and success (14:12; 15:5). Jesus calls across the water asking about food. They confess readily enough that they have caught nothing for all their labors. Jesus bids them cast their net on the right side and immediately they enclose so many fish that they cannot haul them in.

So far, Peter has been pictured as leader and the Beloved Disciple has not even been mentioned. But at the moment of the catch, the author says that the Beloved Disciple reveals to Peter, "It is the Lord" (cf. 13:24–26; 21:20). As faith must precede effective work in the new community, so the Beloved Disciple articulates the fundamental insight and confession, and only then does Peter spring into action. Working nearly naked, he "girded" himself and sprang into the sea, leaving the other six to bring the boat to shore, dragging the net full of fish behind them.

On land they find fish cooking on a charcoal fire and bread there as well. Jesus calls to them to bring some of their catch. Does he not have enough? Does he seek their cooperation?

Peter hauls the net ashore and it is found to contain 153 large fish. One hundred fifty-three is a triangular number, consisting of the sum of all the numbers from 1 to 17. While the meaning of the number is unknown, it seems at the very least to mark the catch as mysterious, full, and perfect. Time and again the evangelist ponders the complex oneness of the Christian community on the basis of the work of Jesus and his disciples (see John 17:20–26, Seventh Sunday of Easter). So here all the fish are brought to Jesus by one boat and by one untorn net (cf. 19:23–24; 10:16; 11:51–52).

Verses 11–13 picture Jesus as providing the catch and feeding his people. Jesus wills and directs the catching of people in passing generations, and he is present and working in those who feed them.

The topic shifts at v. 15. They finish eating and Jesus then addresses Simon Peter with a hard question, repeated three times: "Do you love me?" (The Greek words *agapao* and *phileo* are used as synonyms in vv. 15–17.) Only in John's Gospel is the bond between Jesus and his followers described as love. By putting the question three times, Jesus was really asking, "Will you be my disciple and follow me, whatever the cost?" (cf. 13:31–35; 15:13).

And discipleship does cost. Jesus alludes to the price both in the word "love" and in the use of the metaphor of shepherding. From the beginning "shepherd" has been a standing description of leadership and service in the Christian community (Acts 20:23; Eph. 4:11; 1 Pet. 5:24; 2:25). In speaking to Peter about "feeding" *(bosko)* and "tending" *(poimaino)* the sheep, Jesus conjures up the full range of the shepherd's work: leading to pasture, protecting while grazing, recalling from straying, binding up injuries, providing shelter. But there is more to shepherding than all that good work. In the Fourth Gospel, Jesus is movingly portrayed as the Good Shepherd *(ho poimēn ho kalos)* who laid down his life for the sheep (10:11, 17–18). So feeding and tending the flock means more than performing a few simple acts of care. Jesus summons Peter and other leaders of the church to mortal combat against evil on behalf of the flock of God.

Peter is grieved, not simply to be asked three times, or to be reminded of his three denials by Jesus' three questions; he is grieved as the cost of discipleship dawns on him. Yet he perseveres. He answers correctly and faithfully each time.

At the climax of the dialog (vv. 18–19), Jesus announces that Peter was being bound in two ways: he was being harnessed in discipleship to Jesus, and he would finally be tied as a prisoner with arms stretched out on the crossbeam. That is a hard word for Easter. Allegiance to the Easter Lord means a life of discipleship ("Follow me!" v. 19). All discipleship means surrendering our freedom and sharing our lives with others, trusting that such acts will not destroy but will fulfill our lives (cf. 10:10; 12:24). Not only martyrdom but all discipleship glorifies God, because all discipleship brims with the glorious self-giving of Jesus.

The Fourth Sunday of Easter

Lutheran	Roman Catholic	Episcopal	Common Lectionary
Acts 13:15–16a, 26–33	Acts 13:14, 43–52	Acts 13:15–16, 26–33 (34–39) or Num. 27:12–23	Acts 13:15–16, 26–33
Rev. 7:9–17	Rev. 7:9, 14b–17	Rev. 7:9–17 or Acts 13:15–16, 26–33 (34–39)	Rev. 7:9–17
John 10:22–30	John 10:27–30	John 10:22–30	John 10:22–30

One common element in the lessons this Sunday is attention to the community. Luke reports a sermon of Paul in the synagogue of Pisidian Antioch on the first missionary journey, calling Jews and Gentiles into new community (Acts 13). The seer has a vision of a great multitude clothed in white (Revelation 7). And in John's Gospel

Jesus responds to a question put to him one winter's day on the temple mount in Jerusalem by uttering a short speech on the flock of God (John 10).

Disparate in form, the lessons yet have unity. They share a focus on the nature and boundaries of the people of God. Paul in Acts insists that Gentiles are not excluded. The seer ponders the size and variety of the company of martyrs. Jesus in John's Gospel defines the flock of God as those who hear his voice.

FIRST LESSON: ACTS 13:15–16, 26–33

For reasons unknown to us, John Mark abandoned the first missionary journey at Perga in Pamphylia (the southern coast of Turkey). Barnabas and Paul trudged on, climbing the Taurus Mountains into the high plateau of Anatolia, cradle of ancient Hittite and Phrygian civilizations. They reached Pisidian Antioch and entered the synagogue there on the Sabbath. In a scene reminiscent of Luke 4:16–30, law and prophets were read, and then rulers of the synagogue invited the visitors to speak "any word of exhortation" (cf. 4:36; Heb. 13:22) they might have for the people.

Paul spoke for the two missionaries. He addressed his hearers as Israelites and God-fearers (Acts 13:16), probably two groups: born Jews, and Gentiles who were attracted to Judaism because of its monotheism and ethics but who were not ready to undergo circumcision and become full converts.

Paul rehearsed the deeds of God, beginning with God's choice of the patriarchs and the rescue from the land of Egypt in the days of Moses (vv. 16–17). Then he spoke of entering the land and Samuel's anointing of David, a man after God's own heart (v. 22). Now God has set one of David's descendants on a throne far higher than David ever had. As climax to the whole ancient story of God's way with the world, God has now raised up Jesus from the dead, thereby designating him as royal "Son" (v. 33; cf. Ps. 2:7). He will rule forever as universal "Savior" (v. 23).

That title "Savior" is central to all that Paul is saying, and he sums up his entire speech to that mixed audience of Jews and Gentiles by describing his words as "the message of this salvation" (cf. 10:36–37). The resurrection is the coronation of the Savior-Son. By raising Jesus from the dead, God has established a new sovereignty, far different from David's. It is a new kind of kingdom, full of promise for all who believe, Jews and Gentiles alike. Paul's word of salvation has the power to explode old conceptions of self and world, as well as power to replace them with fresh convictions adding up to a new personal and social reality.

Raised from the dead and ruling, the Savior-King Jesus dispenses the royal gifts of forgiveness and freedom (vv. 38–39). To celebrate Easter means to hail this new Savior-King in faith, and to receive from his hand those shattering gifts. They shatter old alliances, call into question old loyalties, and shake the imagination awake so that we begin to entertain a vision of new community. Celebrating Easter means giving up the old and beginning to practice new and inclusive community of Jews and Gentiles, men and women, young and old.

In three momentous mission journeys Paul crossed geographical boundaries, moving from province to province and from Asia to Europe. He traveled as the agent of Jesus Christ, enthroned by resurrection. It is tempting to portray Paul as a heroic figure and to speak of him as a gifted individual throwing himself into a cause against overwhelming odds.

But Luke would have us see Paul as more than a hero, more even than a courageous proclaimer of words about Jesus' resurrection. Paul embodies resurrection. He lives not a heroic life but new and resurrected life under the lordship of Jesus. His journeys are not pieces in some grand personal project. They are travels undertaken by a man who has stopped trying to destroy life (cf. Acts 9:1) and who has begun to share life. Once he tried to eliminate people but now he embraces them. (See the choice between "a murderer" and "the Author of life" in Acts 3:14–15.) After his encounter with the resurrected Jesus, Paul surrendered his old project and began to surrender his days and his energy on behalf of Jesus' project. Paul's life as reported in Acts is an Easter celebration. He shares life with others, especially with those who differ from him. Easter means crossing hard boundaries separating nations and races, sexes and generations, classes and cultures. Easter means crossing boundaries for the sake of new community in the name of the Author of life.

SECOND LESSON: REVELATION 7:9–17

Last Sunday's reading from Revelation (5:11–14) celebrated Jesus' death as an act of ransoming women and men for God. The entire lection focused on Jesus as Lamb and on the song of the heavenly choir, praising his action.

Now comes a meditation on the ransomed people. In fact, Revelation 7 consists of two great visions of the ransomed: the 144,000 out of the twelve tribes of Israel (7:1–8) and the multitude beyond number (7:9–17). These are two ways of designating the entire body of Christian martyrs. John "heard" (7:4) the martyrs described in traditional biblical terms as the 144,000, and he "looked" and saw (7:9) the innumerable host. As elsewhere (5:5–6), what John sees interprets what he hears in fresh and surprising imagery.

The ransomed stand in the presence of the Throne and the Lamb, robed in white and bearing branches of palm, emblems of purity and victory. They stand and shout: God and the Lamb have won the victory! They have rescued us and brought us safely through!

Heavenly beings take up the chant, answering antiphonally, "Amen" (v. 12). And they bless God with a simple doxology, crediting God with all the words that Roman caesars liked to hear in praise of themselves.

One of the elders poses a question to the seer, and it is really the seer's question to the readers: Who do you imagine will finally stand in the presence of God and of the Lamb, robed in white and flourishing branches of palm, forever alive and savoring divine salvation and victory?

The seer is modest, and the elder answers his own question. The victors are those who have come through (not around) the great tribulation. The details of that tribulation *(thlipsis)* fill other chapters of the Revelation (and other parts of the New Testament as well, since it was widely believed that a final terrible outburst of horrors would precede the final and full victory of God; cf. Mark 13:19). But here the elder concentrates on who came through and how.

They have come safely into the presence of God, because "they have washed their robes and made them white in the blood of the Lamb" (v. 14). These are apparently the martyrs and not the totality of the Christian community. Martyrdom means fidelity all the way to death and is highly prized in Revelation, and yet all these are said to have washed their robes not in their own blood but in the blood of the Lamb. And yet their faithfulness even to death testifies that they have penetrated the secret of the Lamb as Lion (Revelation 5) and understand the contents of the scroll. They grasp the mystery of the power of ransoming love.

In a hymn or poem the elder then speaks of God as king and priest. God's place of dwelling is described both as "the throne" and "the temple." And so God's people, like children of the royal house, live perpetually before the throne of God, and like a body of priests they serve God within the temple. The one who sits upon the throne is their shelter and their dwelling place.

Therefore they shall not want for food or drink (Psalm 23), nor shall the sun strike them by day (Psalm 121). The Lamb will be their

Shepherd (Psalm 23; John 10), leading them to springs of living water (cf. Rev. 22:1–5). And God will wipe away from their eyes all tears of agony or unknowing, endured in faith (21:3–4, Fifth Sunday of Easter).

This lesson is addressed especially to those who are oppressed as they attempt to live their lives in fidelity to God's sovereign rule through Jesus Christ. The persecution of the innocent raises questions in every generation about God's justice, but this lesson announces good news. Easter means victory not just for Jesus but for all who call him Lord. Those who belong to him will share his Easter triumph. Even before that final triumph, those who belong to him rejoice that they stand for righteousness and life in a world that sometimes worships deadly and unrighteous power.

GOSPEL: JOHN 10:22–30

Beginning in chapter 5, the evangelist presents the words and deeds of Jesus in the setting of Jewish festivals: Sabbath, Passover, Tabernacles. Now it is the feast of Dedication or of the Renewal of the Temple, otherwise known as Hanukkah. This wintertime festival (late December) celebrates the victories of the Maccabees over Syrian oppressors and the rededication of the temple after the removal of pagan cult objects. Themes of victory and freedom and the restoration of native Jewish leadership were in the air.

Against that background, in Solomon's portico in the temple at Jerusalem Jesus was asked to state plainly whether he might be the Christ, the Messiah, the leader for whom God's people prayed. That is exactly the same question asked of Jesus in the Synoptic Gospels by priests at his trial. And it is not so different from the question John the Baptist sent from his prison via two disciples (Matt. 11:2–3).

Jesus replies that the works he has done in their midst (his healings and feedings) testify clearly enough. What his questioners need are not more words or deeds but something else. He then begins expounding their unbelief in terms of his prior words on shepherding. He had spoken earlier in the chapter about what distinguishes the good shepherd from mere hired hands, and now he focuses on the sheep. What characterizes the flock?

Jesus says that his questioners do not believe, and implies that they never will (10:25). They have heard his words and witnessed his deeds (cf. Matt. 11:3–5), and all to no effect (John 8:37). They do not believe, and that is the same as saying they do not belong to his flock. Those who are his own know the voice of their shepherd and follow him (10:3–4, 14).

Previously Jesus has said that hirelings care nothing for the sheep, and the thief comes only to destroy, but the good shepherd gives the flock abundant life (10:10). Here he declares that his sheep will never perish nor will any wolf or enemy snatch them out of his hand (v. 28). The flock is forever safe in the hands of Jesus. Immediately Jesus expands that thought by declaring that nothing can snatch the sheep from the Father's hand (v. 29).

Union with God is given through Jesus' words and deeds. All our Gospels describe the sad plight of the sheep before the advent of Jesus. They were scattered and lost (cf. Matt. 9:36). But through Jesus' ministry of words, deeds, and suffering, and through his resurrection and exaltation, the scattered are gathered, the lost are recovered, those languishing in darkness are brought to the light, and the dead are quickened.

Jesus and the Father are one in more ways than one. They are one in their love for the sheep, one in their opposition to death and evil and the lie, one in their determination to bless the sheep with indestructible life, one in their power to free and enliven. The Son is the perfect expression of God in the world. Jesus is the word of God, so that whoever has seen or heard Jesus has seen and heard God. Thus he climaxes his short speech with the saying "The Father and I are one" (cf. John 17, Seventh Sunday of Easter).

The Fifth Sunday of Easter

Lutheran	Roman Catholic	Episcopal	Common Lectionary
Acts 13:44–52	Acts 14:21–27	Acts 13:44–52 or Lev. 19:1–2, 9–18	Acts 14:8–18
Rev. 21:1–5	Rev. 21:1–5a	Rev. 19:1, 4–9 or Acts 13:44–52	Rev. 21:1–6
John 13:31–35	John 13:31–33, 34–35	John 13:31–35	John 13:31–35

What proofs can we offer of the truth of Easter? What arguments can we muster? Luke speaks in Acts of joy and the Holy Spirit. Even in lonely exile, the seer is filled with confidence that God will one day wipe away all tears (Revelation 21). And Jesus, surrounded by the misunderstanding and plots of his enemies and confronted with denial and betrayal among his disciples, points to living by the new commandment of love (John 13). The lections for the Fifth Sunday of Easter offer all these as proofs and evidences of the reality of the resurrection of Jesus. Joy, hope, love, and the Holy Spirit are in fact the most solemn liturgies and highest celebrations of Easter.

FIRST LESSON: ACTS 13:44–52

Paul's words in the synagogue of Pisidian Antioch (Acts 13:16–41, Fourth Sunday of Easter) had a profound effect on the hearers. He and Barnabas were invited to return. The following Sabbath, nearly all of Antioch gathered to hear "the word of God" (13:44). Crowds of Antiochenes, many of them pagans or Gentiles, thronged about the synagogue.

When certain Jews saw those crowds of Gentiles hanging on the words of Paul, they were gripped by "jealousy" (RSV) or zeal for the holiness of God (cf. 5:17). They feared that Paul was assaulting the line between clean and unclean, between Jew and Gentile, and that he would erase it by his proclamation of Jesus as a new way to God's embrace among the people of God. So they began to contradict Paul's words and even to belittle and blaspheme him (v. 45).

Throughout Luke-Acts God's agents proclaim the Word of God at a Jewish or pagan holy place, provoking both faith and hostility. In response to hostility, the agents then move away from the rejecters and reach out with God's word to new audiences. Rejection is interpreted by God's messengers not as defeat or as a sign of the weakness of their message, but as a signal that it is time (on God's clock) to turn to people who were originally beyond the agent's sphere of concern. Rejection by some spells unexpected opportunity for others.

So Paul and Barnabas say that "it was necessary" (a key Lukan motif) that God's word should go first to the Jews. That was God's plan. But now "it is necessary" that the word be offered to the Gentiles. Luke was almost certainly a Gentile. He sees the movement of the message of salvation from Jerusalem to Rome, from Jew to Gentile, not as accidental but as providential. If the Jews, God's ancient people, were blessed with the gift of prophets and the ministry of Jesus, so the Gentiles are now blessed with the gift of Scriptures and the word about Jesus.

So Paul and Barnabas declare, "We turn to the Gentiles" (13:46). And they see that movement prefigured in ancient Scriptures (Isa. 49:6). Originally, the prophet said to Israel that her destiny was not to rule the Gentiles and be rich among the nations as nations count richness. Her calling was to be a light to the nations, distributing spiritual blessings to the Gentiles. Simeon celebrated the birth of Jesus by quoting the same Scripture. Jesus is Israel's glory and a light of revelation to the Gentiles (Luke 2:32; cf. John 8:12; 9:5). Paul here discovers a fresh use for the same prophecy, saying that Christian missionaries are the light of the nations (v. 47). Jesus, in the Sermon on the Mount (Matt. 5:14), calls every disciple to be the light of the world.

The Gentiles rejoiced and "glorified the Word of God" (v. 48). In Acts the Word of God is a divine force barely separable from the person of God. God's powerful Word provokes powerful reactions. Believers received it at Pisidian Antioch and through them it spread rapidly, so that light began to dawn on Gentiles throughout that region (v. 49). And unbelievers were not simply passive. They rose up in active resistance to the Word. They "incited the devout women of high standing and the leading men of the city," so that Paul and Barnabas were driven from the district (v. 50).

The messengers of the Lord "shook off the dust from their feet against them" (Luke 9:5; Acts 18:6; 22:23), a gesture of contempt signaling their judgment that those persecutors were unclean and unworthy. The believers in Antioch were "filled with joy and with the Holy Spirit" (v. 52). And Paul and Barnabas continued their march, moving down the road toward Iconium.

In *Habits of the Heart* Robert Bellah and his associates comment on widespread amnesia among middle-class Americans. We have forgotten the stories that shaped the values and the lives of the founders of our nation. One of the two lost stories is the biblical narrative. Because it is largely unknown, people lack a language for describing their aspirations and the highest stirrings of their hearts. We fall back on other stories to interpret our lives, and most of the alternative stories glorify the individual who works hard to overcome adversity and achieve a lonely success. If we are to recover a sense of peoplehood and community, we must recover our stories.

In the lections of the Fourth and Fifth Sundays of Easter, Luke portrays Paul and Barnabas telling the story that stretches all the way back to Abraham and Moses, through Samuel and David, down to the resurrection of Jesus. That story is all about God's struggle to shape a community of people, generation after generation. The resurrection of Jesus is a great turning point in the story. After Jesus' death and resurrection new tribes and nations are invited to enter the community and make the continuing story their own. They are summoned to root their lives in the soil of that history and let it nurture them and give them meaning.

Within the community new believers found "joy and the Holy Spirit" (Acts 13:52). Sustained by the power of that Spirit, Paul and Barnabas continued their journey to ventures the ending of which they could not see, "by paths as yet untrodden, through perils unknown." As they went, they both told the story and wrote new pages.

SECOND LESSON: REVELATION 21:1–6

In the last two chapters of the Book of Revelation, John peers beyond human history with all its persecutions and apostasies, its bravery and martyrdoms. He sees the goal, the new heaven and the new earth, and he reports his vision.

The first heaven and the first earth, seemingly so stable, with apparently permanent pleasures and powers, have vanished. And the sea, ancient symbol of rebellious powers arrayed against the creator (cf. Rev. 13:1), likewise ceased to be.

The focus of the seer's vision is then a city, an altogether new Jerusalem, descending from the creator's hand fresh and spotless, like a bride adorned for her husband (21:2). God has prepared not just a new world but a place of human habitation, a home for a new community of women and men under God.

Barriers between God and humankind drop away. Separation caused by doubt or persecution ceases. No human voice but "a great voice from the throne" declares that God will dwell in the midst of the people (v. 3). In the presence of the God of resurrection and life, pain and death will have no place. God will personally wipe dry every tear-stained face (7:17; Isa. 25:6–8).

Once more, for the first time since Rev. 1:8, the Lord God speaks to John. In the beginning the heavenly voice had said, "I am the Alpha and the Omega" (cf. 21:6). Now here at the end, neither an elder nor an angel nor the seer, but rather "the One who sat upon the throne" declares, "Behold, I make all things new" (v. 5).

That same voice of God commands the seer to publish this good news, "for these words are trustworthy and true" (v. 5) in spite of all the evidence of our eyes and bodies, battered daily by countless pieces of contrary evidence. Revelation, like all parts of the New Testament, extols the power of words written and words spoken. In fact, Revelation begins with a benediction on the lector (1:3) and concludes with a tough warning to all hearers of these words (22:18–19).

The seer asserts that his vision of God's coming victory is true and people can count on it, because the Lord God and no other is "the Alpha and the Omega," the beginning and the end (1:8).

The visions of Revelation are sometimes exotic, even bizarre, and frequently disturbing. But they merit our attention. They enshrine the sharpest criticisms of secularism and of lukewarm discipleship to be found in the New Testament, and they also voice the powerful hope of an entirely new world to come.

GOSPEL: JOHN 13:31–35

This lection is the opening paragraph of Jesus' Farewell Discourse (13:31—17:26). Here Jesus speaks not only to the Twelve (or Eleven) on the Thursday evening of his last week on earth but also to the community of believers of all times and all places. And he speaks about the high mystery of his cross. That mystery is so difficult and so contrary to all ordinary calculations that it evokes both revulsion and trust, both the response of Judas and that of the Beloved Disciple and Peter.

At his final meal with his disciples, Jesus rose from the table, laid aside his outer robes, bound his waist with a towel, poured water into a basin, and washed his disciples' feet (13:1–5). Jesus then interpreted his strange action. His life was poured out to cleanse and sanctify the world (vv. 6–10) and was offered up as an example of humble service (vv. 11–20). Immediately afterward, Jesus offered his troubling prophecy of betrayal by one of the Twelve (13:21–30). Judas took the morsel and departed into the darkness, and Jesus began then to speak once more of his own departure.

In all four Gospels, but especially in John's Gospel, Jesus foresees his death and spells out its consequences for his community. After washing his disciples' feet, Jesus declares that everything is now ready for "the Son of man," the world's judge, to be "glorified" (v. 31). Jesus is talking about his dying. But how can it be a glorification? Isn't death base and mean, the defeat of life? Isn't it the ultimate humiliation suffered by every living thing?

From the beginning of his Gospel, the Fourth Evangelist has been mulling over the meanings of Jesus' dying. And whatever else it may be it is victory. His cross is the first step on the path of his return to God from whom he came out. His shed blood is a cleansing flood, enabling sinners to step into the presence of God. In his dying we see in concentrated form the love he has for the world (13:1). Every act of love praises God, but this act of love, offered upon the cross, praises God most highly. Every deed of love pleases God, but God looks with deepest favor on the love Jesus displayed at the cross.

Jesus and God are glorified at the cross. Jesus is lifted up and God is honored. And God glorifies Jesus by receiving him into the glorious union of oneness with God. The Word spoken into the world in the incarnation (John 1:1–18) is received back into the life of God at the cross.

In this lection Jesus begins to speak of his disciples and of all believing readers as "little children," and with warmth and tenderness gathers them close about him like a parent about to depart in death. Jesus declares that he will remain with the disciples in ordinary visible fellowship for a short time only. His death is imminent. He will be removed from their midst, and they will seek him. They will be filled with sorrow at his departure and wish he were still with them in all the old ways. They do not yet understand the importance of his cross, and they will grieve for a time because of it.

At this moment they do not want to be separated from him and would go with him, but he goes his glorious pathway first, without them. They must not try to extend the old fellowship but must begin to learn new connections with him.

This is the moment for "a new commandment" (v. 34). The commandment is new not in the sense that it is number eleven and is added to an old ten, nor even that it is new in spirit and replaces the old ten (cf. Lev. 19:18). It is new because a new age dawns when Jesus mounts up to God via the cross, because the Son of man links heaven and earth in fresh ways, opening up new access to God and the life of God.

The commandment is new because it flows from the new oneness between earth and heaven established by that awesome love at the cross. Love like that of Jesus at the cross means the pouring of the immortal and astonishing life of God into the historical and earth-bound life of humanity.

Humans both yearn for love and fear to love, afraid that loving others, especially loving strangers or enemies, will mean being diminished and impoverished. We fear that loving will mean loss of power and loss of life. But Jesus' words in this lection declare that the outpouring of his life in love at the cross means not loss but great gain, not defeat but glory.

As he embarks on the path that leads to his own cross and glory, Jesus calls disciples to "love one another" (v. 34). Loving words and loving actions are the vital signs of discipleship (v. 35). Indeed, love is the purest celebration of Easter.

The Sixth Sunday of Easter

Lutheran	Roman Catholic	Episcopal	Common Lectionary
Acts 14:8–18	Acts 15:1–2, 22–29	Acts 14:8–18 or Joel 2:21–27	Acts 15:1–2, 22–29
Rev. 21:10–14, 22–23	Rev. 21:10–14, 22–23	Rev. 21:22— 22:5 or Acts 14:8–18	Rev. 21:10, 22–27
John 14:23–29	John 14:23–29	John 14:23–29	John 14:23–29

Where is God? What is the dwelling place of the living God? Is it a historical community of Jews and Gentiles, women and men, old and young, united by the action of God their Creator (Acts 15)? Is it the New Jerusalem of hope, which needs neither sun nor temple because the incandescence of God's own presence fills that holy city (Revelation 21)? Or is the heart of the individual believer-lover the dwelling place of God in Christ (John 14)?

The lessons for this Sunday offer these three answers to the question, Where is God? These responses are not in competition with one another. They represent the spiritual visions of three individuals captured in three different ways by the power of the one Risen Lord. These visions stand in criticism of all our lesser dreams and visions, and they serve also to stretch our moral imaginations and stoke our hope.

FIRST LESSON: ACTS 15:1–2, 22–29

Acts 15 deals with the Apostolic Council or Jerusalem Conference. The chapter comes almost exactly at the midpoint of the narrative, and the great names are all present: James, Peter, and Paul. They handle great issues confronting the early church: Are circumcision and the dietary laws binding as Word of God on all people and for all time? Are Jew and Gentile to continue as two peoples or can they possibly be one under God?

Answers that may seem obvious to us were far from clear to the participants. At first, to be a Christian meant to be a Jew with a few peculiar beliefs about Jesus. Christian Jews continued to attend synagogue and temple, to celebrate Sabbath and all the festivals, to observe the Law in all its details as part of their joyous service to God.

Preachers like Paul, however, began to reach out to Gentiles and found a ready hearing among them. Gentiles in great numbers abandoned idols, confessed Jesus as "Lord," sealed their penitence and faith in baptism and began to serve the living God. And Paul accepted them into the Christian fellowship without demanding circumcision or the keeping of the Law of Moses. Was Paul's program a personal whim? Or did it enjoy the backing of God?

Agreement was not easy. For a time the Christian community at Antioch (in Syria) was marked by a free and open spirit, fully supporting Paul. Jewish and Gentile Christians formed one fellowship. They ate at one table as peers and partners under God, not on the basis of the Law but in spite of the Law, on the basis of a shared faith.

Practice in Antioch was shocking to some conservative Christian Jews of Jerusalem. When they visited Antioch, they taught the necessity of circumcision. Without it, they said, no one can be saved (15:1). Paul and Barnabas debated the issue with them and finally the whole matter was referred to Jerusalem (15:2), which throughout Acts enjoys unique standing as mother church of the Christian movement. It was the place where "the apostles and the elders" resided.

Paul and Barnabas traveled south from Antioch to Jerusalem. Luke describes their journey as a kind of triumphal procession. News of the conversion of Gentiles "gave great joy to all the brethren" (v. 3) along the way, and they were warmly welcomed even at Jerusalem by the apostles and the elders (v. 4).

At Jerusalem, pious Jewish Christian believers, sharing the Pharisees' devotion to the Law, repeated their views concerning Gentile converts: They must be circumcised, and they must keep the Law of Moses in its entirety (v. 5). They believed that to be a Christian is to be a Jew, albeit a new kind.

The debate was joined (v. 6). Peter rehearsed his own experiences in the case of Cornelius, offering a kind of summary of Acts 10 and 11. God had freely accepted the Gentile Cornelius with all household (v. 9), without circumcision and Law. Then Peter went on to describe the Law as an unbearable yoke, so full of ordinances that it cannot be observed perfectly (v. 10). He concluded by saying that both Jews and Gentiles have access to God on the basis of "the grace of the Lord Jesus" (v. 11).

Then (v. 12) Barnabas and Paul recount their experiences among the Gentiles of central Asia Minor (narrated in Acts 13—14). Finally, James addressed the assembly (v. 13). Not heard from previously in Acts, his words are given more space here than those of the other participants. He finds warrant in Scripture (Amos 9:11–12) for the promise of the ingathering of the Gentiles.

So Luke pictures Peter and James, the great leaders of the first generation of apostles, as standing in invincible agreement with Paul and Barnabas. All together oppose the view that Gentiles must be circumcised and observe the Law of Moses.

Delegates were chosen and a letter was drafted to publish the results of the conference. Judas Barabbas (cf. 1:23) and Silas (= Silvanus, 1 Thess. 1:1), leaders in the Jerusalem Christian community, were dispatched to Antioch along with Paul and Barnabas (v. 22). In the letter and oral messages "the apostles and elders" of Jerusalem dissociated themselves from the hard-liners who had upset the Antioch Christians (v. 24). Barnabas and Paul are praised as "beloved" and as workers who have "risked their lives for the sake of the Lord Jesus Christ" (vv. 25–26).

Then four prohibitions are named as "necessary" for the unity of Jewish and Gentile believers in the community. They are not necessary for entrance into the community or for salvation. First, converted pagans should "abstain from the pollutions of idols" (15:20) or "from what has been sacrificed to idols" (15:29). They are not to participate any longer in pagan sacrificial meals or in the cults of other gods. The church was to be as fiercely antipagan as the synagogue.

Second, they must abstain "from blood"; and third, they must abstain from "what is strangled." These two prohibitions mean avoiding the meat of animals killed by strangulation, because the blood would not have drained off (Lev. 17:10–16).

Fourth, Gentile converts must also abstain from "unchastity" (15:20, 29), from sexual license in general and also from marriage to close relatives (Lev. 18:6–18) and mixed marriages with pagans (2 Cor. 6:14). Monogamy and family life were to be respected in the church as in the synagogue.

All three prohibitions aim at enabling Jews and Gentiles to live at peace in a single community, and to eat at a single table. For the Gentile Christians to act otherwise would have meant the creation of two churches rather than one. The goal of oneness can often be achieved only when brothers and sisters are willing to yield a portion of their freedom for the sake of others. Trusting the crucified as Lord empowers a joyous yielding for the sake of community rather than mere grudging compromises undertaken for the sake of peace and quiet.

SECOND LESSON: REVELATION 21:10–14, 22–27

One of the seven angels summoned the seer, promising a vision of "the Bride, the wife of the Lamb" (21:10). Again, what is heard is interpreted by what is seen (cf. 5:5–6; 7:4, 9). The angel spoke of the Bride but showed the seer "the holy city Jerusalem," descending from heaven as gift of God (21:10).

The new Jerusalem shines with the glory of God, and the seer describes that brilliance and light in terms of hard gems and geometrical proportions, gates of pearl and boulevard of pure gold, in a valiant effort to communicate its exquisite wonder and perfection (21:11–21).

More satisfying, more mysterious, more suggestive of spiritual and moral splendors, are the concluding words of the lection (21:22–27). The new city has no temple. The new city and the new earth no longer need that symbol of the presence of God, that bridgehead of holiness in a fallen world, for the Lord God and the Lamb will perfectly indwell that city, filling it with holiness.

Furthermore, sun and moon, those great first-created lamps, are needed no more. For "the glory of God is the light of that city, and the Lamb is its lamp" (v. 23; cf. John 8:12; 9:5). God and the Lamb are light enough, and that city will be so full of light (cf. Matt. 5:14–16) that its light will illumine the path of nations (v. 24a).

At the beginning of Revelation (1:5) Jesus was named the ruler of the kings of the earth. Here at the end kings stream to the new Jerusalem, offering their wealth to glorify that city (cf. Matt. 2:11), as once they carried their treasures to Rome, enriching that city set on seven hills (vv. 24–26). Up to this point in the Book of Revelation the seer has heaped scorn on the riches of the world (cf. chap. 18) and has predicted the world's destruction. Now he seems to soften his tough stand against the world and all its goods and artifacts. He appears to say that the world will be not destroyed but reordered, so that everything good in the products and cultures of the nations will shine in a new light and will be used to glorify God and to enrich the life of the people of God.

The gates of that new city need never be shut (v. 25). They stand wide open in peace and hospitality to people ransomed from every tribe and tongue and nation. Its open gates are the open arms of God extending a universal welcome. Excluded are all things unclean and false (Isa. 52:1). Only those may hope to enter whose names are inscribed in "the Lamb's book of life" (v. 27; cf. 3:5; 17:8). That book is the register on which are written the names of all the citizens of that new city.

The seer offers a vision full of strong hope. The actual cities of human history, even the most celebrated centers of commerce and culture, are marred by poverty and scarred by crime. Political and economic systems promise prosperity but seem inevitably to produce misery for many citizens who are driven to the margins of society and denied a decent life. At times the systems devised by men and women to govern their lives together seem to be breaking down and history seems to be plunging toward final destruction. But the seer declares that the goal of history is not ruin but a new city, the new Jerusalem. The sovereignty of the God who raised Jesus Christ from the dead is moving toward a new human society under God's gracious rule. Celebrating Easter means trusting that vision, so that hopelessness and moral lethargy are overcome and we find energy to set up in our old cities signs of the new city of God.

GOSPEL: JOHN 14:23-29

Jesus had spoken of his dying as his going away to the Father's house (14:2-3). As earthly monarchs inhabit large dwellings, so God in heaven can also be portrayed as living in a huge palace with rooms beyond number. Jesus says that he goes before his disciples to prepare a place for them in the Father's house (14:2).

Jesus uses that homely imagery like a text and then proceeds to elaborate and modify it in the remainder of John 14. As his disciples raise questions and reveal misconceptions (14:5-11), Jesus utters fundamental encouragement: "I will never leave you desolate" (the Greek word is *orphanous*; the English "orphaned" captures the sense exactly; 14:18). Beyond the cross and a few resurrection appearances will come a time when they will no longer see him. But then he promises: "I will come to you" (v. 18). How and when?

Jesus is not here speaking of his final coming on clouds with angels and trumpet fanfare. Instead, he speaks the language of spiritual indwelling. By death he withdraws from the world of touch and sight and enters directly into the presence of God. Henceforth, he says, "I am in my Father" (14:20). But not only is Jesus "going home" to God; he says that the time is close at hand when the disciples will be in Jesus and Jesus will be in the disciples (14:20). In fact, Jesus and the Father will come and make their home in Jesus' followers, described in John 14 as believers (vv. 10-11) and lovers (vv. 15-23).

At 14:25 Jesus begins to talk of the Divine Presence beyond Good Friday and Easter in terms of the work of the Paraclete (the Counselor or Advocate, the Holy Spirit). The Paraclete will continue the ministry of Jesus. The Paraclete will not produce something different from what Jesus taught but will come in Jesus' name, teaching disciples all things (v. 26) by bringing clarity to their minds and hearts about all that Jesus had revealed or attempted to reveal to them.

To the disciple, initiated into the meanings of Jesus' death, his departure should therefore not be troubling and disturbing (14:1). He leaves in order to bind disciples even closer to himself and to God. And that means peace, not as the world understands it, but it is peace nonetheless, and his peace drives out all fear (v. 27; cf. 20:19–26).

So finally (in 14:28) the first words of the chapter (14:2–3) are paraphrased and repeated: "I go away, and I will come to you." Disciples and readers should now be able to see that he was not talking about literal palaces in the sky but about reentering the heart of the divine life from which he had come forth in the beginning. Therefore his dying is not his finish. He returns to God who sent him, because the commission he had received from God is now complete.

Jesus had received the task of loving the world, lost and scattered in its darkness, back into oneness with God (cf. John 3:16; 11:52). The cross is not the defeat of God's commission but its enactment, and God is "greater than I," says Jesus (v. 28). The love poured out at the cross is not merely the sacrifice of an isolated, kindly, ancient individual named Jesus. It is the doing of the undying and omnipotent God.

To the unbelieving eye Jesus' "going away" on the cross looks like the destruction of Jesus. But the eye of faith sees better. At the cross Jesus completes the task, given by the heavenly Father, of pouring divine love into the world (see 13:1). And the cross releases Jesus from earthly limitations, so that he is freed to come to disciples as godly energy and presence, fulfilling God's desire to dwell with people and to have them dwell in the divine presence. Celebrating Easter means celebrating the presence of God in self and in neighbor.

The Ascension of Our Lord

Lutheran	Roman Catholic	Episcopal	Common Lectionary
Acts 1:1–11	Acts 1:1–11	Acts 1:1–11 or 2 Kings 2:1–15	Acts 1:1–11
Eph. 1:16–23	Eph. 1:17–23	Eph. 1:15–23 or Acts 1:1–11	Eph. 1:15–23
Luke 24:44–53	Luke 24:46–53	Luke 24:49–53 or Mark 16:9–15, 19–20	Luke 24:46–53 or Mark 16:9–16, 19–20

Each of our readings speaks of Jesus' "going up" from earth to heaven, from life on earth to new life with God. But each makes it clear that Ascension means far more than upward motion through vast physical distances. Ascension declares the universal Lordship of Jesus in the power of God's Spirit (Acts 1). It means the overthrow of divisive forces and the creation of new alignments among women and men of all nations (Ephesians 1). Ascension inaugurates the rule of Christ, whose presence is purest blessing (Luke 24).

FIRST LESSON: ACTS 1:1–11

In the opening paragraph of Acts, Luke seems to look back on the ministry of Jesus and to speak of the apostles as revered figures of a bygone era. Nevertheless the present connection with that past time is secure, because of links deliberately forged by Jesus. Jesus chose the Twelve through the Spirit (Acts 1:2), kept them close around him as witnesses of his words and deeds in Galilee and Jerusalem, and then appeared to them after his resurrection, eating with them and demonstrating his victory over death and the grave (Luke 24; Acts 1:3–4; 10:41). Indeed, for forty days after Easter Jesus himself instructed them on the topic of "the kingdom of God" in order to prepare them for their own ministry of the Word of God.

But instruction is only one part of their preparation. Jesus commanded the apostles to remain in Jerusalem and to await the empowering gift of the Holy Spirit (1:4–5).

It takes both powerful instruction and the might of the Spirit of God to prepare the apostles. After the triumph of Easter they were full of hope, but their hope was nationalistic and narrow (v. 6): "Lord, will you at this time restore the kingdom to Israel?" They looked for an early renewal of their nation and its ancient glory.

Jesus, however, discourages all date setting and defines the kingship of God in terms of the Holy Spirit, not in terms of the number of men under arms, or the number of weapons in the stockpile. And who will inherit the coming kingdom? God intends to restore "all things" (Acts 3:21), and those who are called to the kingdom are not in Jerusalem and Judea only but in Samaria and as far away as the ends of the earth. Jews, Samaritans, Gentiles will all stream in through the gates to the kingdom God is preparing.

God will do more than simply restore the old Davidic kingdom. The kingdom of God is not a political entity to rival or overshadow Rome and the Parthians. It is altogether different. Jesus is the Lord, but he does not proceed like Persian kings and Roman caesars. Through gracious words, the testimony of chosen witnesses, Jesus invites people everywhere in every age to acknowledge his lordship and to call on his name.

At the end of the forty days of instruction, Jesus was taken up into heaven (cf. Luke 24:51). He has gone up in rank and sits at the right hand, as world ruler chosen and appointed by God.

The ascension of Jesus echoes the ascension of the prophet Elijah (2 Kings 2). Elijah had chosen Elisha as his successor. Elisha wanted to receive a "double measure" (the firstborn's share of the inheritance) of Elijah's spirit. Elisha wished to be designated clearly as Elijah's heir and successor (2 Kings 2:9; Deut. 21:17). Elijah said that Elisha would so inherit but only on one condition, that he have eyes to see Elijah ascending (2 Kings 2:10).

Luke emphasizes with five different verbs and nouns (Acts 1:9–11) that the apostles saw Jesus ascending. They see and acknowledge his lordship, and so they are ready to receive the Spirit of Jesus and to work as the earthly agents of Jesus.

Suddenly two "men" wearing white robes (1:10; cf. Luke 9:30; 24:4) stood by the disciples. They call the disciples to turn from "gazing into heaven" and to take up their mission of proclamation.

Celebrating Easter and Ascension means confessing Jesus as Lord and sharing the gracious word of invitation to his kingdom. His is a peaceable kingdom, embracing women and men of every generation and nation, every race and class. As such it is a powerful alternative to all tyrannies founded on force of arms and to all governments dependent on economic or social discrimination.

Heralding that sovereignty and living as its citizens is the task of the church until Jesus reappears as Lord and Judge.

SECOND LESSON: EPHESIANS 1:15–23

These nine verses constitute one long sentence in Greek. It echoes the preceding paragraph (vv. 3–14) and urges the readers, described as saints in 1:1, to claim as their own the gifts there enumerated, showered upon them freely by God in Christ.

They are already believers and lovers, and Paul is thankful for that. But in the context of thanksgiving he prays for them. His prayer rises on their behalf to "the God of our Lord Jesus Christ" (v. 17). He asks that God would share with them the spiritual gift of wisdom so that veils might fall away and they would have deep and sure knowledge of God (v. 17; cf. 1 Cor. 13:12); and that, knowing God, they might see the goal to which God has called them, namely, the wonder and wealth of being children of God in union with the whole family of God (v. 18). What the author has in mind is the new unity of Jews and Gentiles in Jesus Christ, but he will not speak of "Jews" or "Gentiles" until 2:11.

He prays that they may be grasped as he himself has been by a vision of the new situation created by "the immeasurable greatness of his power" (v. 19) at work in believers. That spiritual power is the same "great might" (v. 19) or divine energy that raised Christ from the grave and exalted him to his seat at God's right hand (v. 20).

Christ's resurrection and ascension undergirds a new vision and fresh relations in human communities. Why? Because his exaltation marks a new age, a shifting of the aeons. Old powers, loyalties, and alignments are suddenly obsolete. Old traditions give way. What once was unthinkable is now a fact. And the new is not something believers must strive to build but is something given. They only need to open their hands and hearts to receive it.

Fresh energies are at work in the world and in the community of believers, and the author celebrates the new in a great doxology (1:20–23). Christ's resurrection means not only that he has broken out of death's grip but that he has been enthroned at God's right hand (Psalm 110), exalted "far above all rule and authority and power and dominion" (v. 21) in the spiritual spheres of heaven or in the political sphere on the earth. He is exalted also "above every name that is named" (v. 21) whether in fear or adoring salute. And he holds that supreme position now and for all the days to come.

God has placed "all things" (v. 22) beneath Christ's feet. God has made Jesus the "head" or ruler of the entire universe, and all his authority he wields "for the church," on behalf of a new humanity.

Christ is the head, his enemies are under his feet, and the church is "his body" (v. 22). As "body," the church acts under the orders and by the energies of the "head." As climax to all that has been said so far, the church or body is now called Christ's "fullness." The church is the instrument of Christ's self-manifestation in the world, the visible expression of the invisible Christ.

The church really celebrates Easter and Ascension when Christ fills the church so that it brims with the restless power of his own loving vitality. Then the church enters indeed into its inheritance as blessed and blessing (1:3), living in praise of the loving energy of God (1:5–6), agent of unity and community (1:10), breaking down old barriers and making peace among the peoples (2:11–22).

GOSPEL: LUKE 24:46–53

Deeply embedded in the mind and plan of God, according to Luke, are these two things: First, the suffering and subsequent exaltation of the Messiah, and second, the universal summons to repent and receive the forgiveness of sins.

The work of God in Jesus erupted in the very heart of Judaism, and the Gospel of Luke ends as it began not only among the Jewish people but in Jerusalem, and not only in Jerusalem but in the temple. And yet Jesus is both the glory of his people Israel and a light of revelation to the Gentiles (2:32) and that means that God reaches out through Jesus to embrace nothing less than "all nations" (24:47; cf. Matt. 28:19).

Jesus commissions the church to bear witness to the plan of God, and describes the equipment the church will require in its task: "Power from on high" (v. 49), and that means the unearthly power of the Spirit of God. The disciples are to wait in Jerusalem until they are "clothed" with that power, as Elisha was "clothed" with the mantle of Elijah.

The scene shifts from Jerusalem proper to Bethany somewhere on the slopes of the Mount of Olives near Bethphage (cf. 19:28–37). Jesus lifted his hands in priestly benediction, supplying a blessing, which Zechariah at the opening of the Gospel had failed to do (1:21–22). Only then, after fully blessing them, did Jesus part from his disciples (v. 51).

Early in Luke 24, confusion, sorrow, and unbelief nearly overwhelmed the disciples (24:4, 11, 17, 25). Throughout the chapter the resurrected Jesus acted to explain and encourage, so that by the end faith and joy prevail (24:31, 34, 52). At the beginning, the disciples see only the grave and the power of death (24:1, 11), but at the end they see blessing and great tasks awaiting them. The disciples returned to Jerusalem, praising God.

The progress of the disciples in this chapter is a message of hope for followers in every generation and place. The living Christ still blesses with life and promises energy sufficient for the church's high calling. That task is the invitation to "all nations" (v. 47) to become one new human family under the hands of Christ upraised in blessing.

The Seventh Sunday of Easter

Lutheran	Roman Catholic	Episcopal	Common Lectionary
Acts 16:6–10	Acts 7:55–60	Acts 16:16–34 or 1 Sam. 12:19–24	Acts 16:16–34
Rev. 22:12–17, 20	Rev. 22:12–14, 16–17, 20	Rev. 22:12–14, 16–17, 20 or Acts 16:16–34	Rev. 22:12–14, 16–17, 20
John 17:20–26	John 17:20–26	John 17:20–26	John 17:20–26

It takes no genius to see problems. It is a simple matter to find parallels today to the ills named in and near our texts: greed and exploitation of unfortunates, crowds and officials aroused by lies and rumors (Acts 16), "dogs, sorcerers, fornicators, murderers, idolaters and liars" (Rev. 22:15), "the world" which fails to "know" God (John 17).

Our texts do more, however, than note evils. They point to the resurrection of the crucified Jesus, and they proclaim Easter not only as victory for Jesus but as victory for the followers of Jesus. And through the lives of Jesus' followers, Easter may become victory also for the world.

Easter means liberation from demons and from bondage of every kind, both in the midst of history (Acts 16) and at the end of all the ages (Revelation 22). Easter means being caught up into the life of God from all places of our being scattered and lost, so that the life of God moves in and through us (John 17).

FIRST LESSON: ACTS 16:16–34

Paul and his party, Luke tells us, had been traveling steadily westward through Asia Minor and were led without their planning but by the nudgings of the Spirit to Troas on the western coast, where Paul in a vision of the night saw a man of Macedonia beckoning him to cross the sea from Asia to Europe (Acts 16:1–6). They dutifully sailed via Samothrace to Neapolis and from that port walked ten miles up the old Roman road to Philippi, leading city of Macedonia and Roman colony. Paul's first convert was a wealthy businesswoman named Lydia (16:11–15), and his first serious recorded conflict in Philippi occurred over a demon-possessed girl (16:16–18).

Luke loves to recount stories exposing the crass motives of opponents of the Christian movement. Time and again he discredits opposition by uncovering motives of greed, as he does here (cf. 1:18;

5:1–11; 19:24; 24:26). Luke specializes in reminding readers that wealth is no infallible indicator of moral or spiritual health (see, e.g., Luke 1:52–53; 16:19–31).

A slave-girl at Philippi was believed to be possessed by the god Apollo, whose symbol was the snake (the girl is described in Greek as "pythonic") and whose business was telling the future. The girl's owners charged a fee for her prophecies and revelations (16:19; cf. 19:24).

On seeing Paul and his companions, that demon-possessed girl cried out, "These men are servants of the most high God and proclaim the way of salvation" (v. 17). Neither Jesus (Luke 4:34) nor Paul desired the advertisements of evil spirits, and both liberated those who were possessed by them. However, by curing the girl Paul destroyed her market value and outraged her owners. Deprived of easy money, the girl's owners stirred public resentment and official action against Paul and Silas, playing on anti-Jewish and pro-Roman sentiment in the marketplace. Philippi was a Roman colony, settled by veterans of the Roman army. The girl's owners cannily played to the gallery, accusing the missionaries of disturbing the peace of the city and making propaganda for exotic and oriental practices deemed unlawful for proud Romans (vv. 19–21).

Peace was indeed disturbed in the city that day. The crowd turned into an ugly mob, and the magistrates themselves tore the clothes from the missionaries and ordered them to be beaten with rods and thrown into jail (vv. 22–24; cf. Luke 23:16, 22; 2 Cor. 11:24–25). The missionaries were consigned to an inner cell with their legs secured in stocks.

Peace restored, the city slept. But Paul and Silas were awake, not groaning in their pain but "singing hymns to God" (v. 25). Other prisoners heard them singing, and so did God, who at midnight answered the hymns with an earthquake (4:31), shaking the prison and shattering fetters (cf. Acts 27:27; Luke 11:5). The jailer woke in a sweat. Fearing that all the prisoners had escaped and that he would be held accountable (cf. 12:19; 27:42), he quickly determined to take his own life and end his career honorably (v. 27). The voice of Paul, however, rang out and reassured the jailer that no prisoners had fled (v. 28).

Now acknowledging Paul and Silas as agents of some powerful God, the jailer threw himself at their feet (v. 29). He had experienced the shattering of his old world and the presence of something totally new in the presence of these missionaries. He cried out, "What must I do to be saved?" (see 2:37; 9:6; 22:10). They invited him, "Believe in the Lord Jesus Christ" (v. 31). And they proclaimed the Word of the Lord to him and his household, his family and servants (v. 32). Then they exchanged gifts. The jailer washed them and their wounds, and the missionaries washed him and his family in baptism (v. 33). The jailer set food before them, and all together rejoiced at table in the presence of God (cf. Luke 24:30–31, 41–42).

Everywhere in Luke-Acts witnesses to Jesus and his resurrection encounter both determined opposition and startling welcome. The news of Easter rubs against the grain of ordinary calculation and challenges old arrangements. Hearers are forced to make hard choices. Often they choose to stick with old alignments, old securities, and old idols. But wherever the power of Easter breaks through, it unites people in a new community of equals under God. That is exactly what happened when the jailer and his prisoners ceased being enemies and became one new family at midnight in Philippi. Both the jailer with his household and Paul with Silas had been bound by chains of varying sorts. And the power of Easter liberated all of them and bound them with bonds of love as brothers and sisters.

SECOND LESSON: REVELATION 22:12–14, 16–17, 20

When will the promises of Revelation come true? The seer has had his visions, but how long must we wait till vision becomes reality?

To the question of "when" at least two answers can be given: (1) Now. The words and visions of Revelation describe not only how things will be but how they already are. God and not Caesar is enthroned above all things. God and no other is the source and goal of the life and breath in all living creatures. God is maker and lover and judge. (2) Soon. From the outset, Revelation has insisted that all the convolutions and vagaries, the progress and horrors of human history, will come to rest at the feet of Jesus Christ, at the throne and judgment seat of God—soon (v. 12).

The Book of Revelation is a marvel of reserve in its descriptions of God. Rich and thick are the descriptions of activities and beings around the heavenly throne, but God is simply "the One seated upon the throne" (4:2). Only twice in the entire book does God speak, and then only very briefly. And each time, at beginning and at end, the brief utterance includes the self-description: "I am the Alpha and the Omega" (1:8; 21:6).

Now here in the concluding verses of the book, this majestic title is found in the mouth of Jesus (v. 13), for Jesus dwells forever in absolute oneness with God. And what we see and hear in Jesus, in his love and teaching and suffering and resurrection, is nothing less than the heart of God.

Seven beatitudes punctuate the Book of Revelation (1:3; 14:13; 16:15; 19:9; 20:6; 22:7, 14). The seventh and last is this word of our lesson (v. 14): "Blessed are those who wash their robes" (cf. 1:5; 7:9, 13). Only they may approach the tree of life (2:7; 22:2; Gen. 2:9) walking boldly through the gates of that holy city. Seven woes and seven bowls of wrath may seem more characteristic of Revelation than the seven beatitudes. And yet the whole of Revelation is meant for blessing. And a beatitude is a powerful utterance, both here in Revelation and in the Sermon on the Mount (Matt. 5:3–12). A beatitude is an ecstatic exclamation, full of power to enthrall and bind in that bondage to God which is perfect liberty.

Excluded from most lectionaries is v. 15, itself a hard word of exclusion. In describing outsiders it descends to mere name-calling, and those ancient names seem superficial ánd harsh. But the whole lection speaks not only of time but also of judgment, of decision, of division. Jesus is coming soon with "recompense," and that means with rewards and punishments, with blessing and woe (v. 12).

The book is coming to an end, and Jesus sets his seal on its testimony, declaring that it has been given by his own specially commissioned messenger (v. 16). He speaks of himself as "root and offspring of David," mighty ruler of the people of God, and he is "bright morning star," harbinger of God's new and dawning day (v. 16).

The Spirit rouses the church (v. 17) to cry its response to the promise of Jesus: "Come!" (1 Cor. 16:22). The members of the church cry out to the Lord, and they cry to one another, encouraging each other to come to the One who alone can quench their spiritual thirst.

What is coming? Our age seems peculiarly burdened by the specter of looming catastrophe: nuclear holocaust, the greenhouse effect, or plague of incurable disease. But the seer looks beyond all present darkness, never denying its reality but seeing farther. What is coming? The new Jerusalem (Revelation 21—22). Who is coming? The Lord God Almighty and the Lamb are coming (21:22; 22:20), and death will be no more, and the former things (now so burdensome) will have passed away (21:4).

Celebrating Easter means living in hope, living in fellowship with all who have "washed their robes" (22:14), and living with moral courage (22:15).

GOSPEL: JOHN 17:20–26

Just as money can lose its purchasing power, so words that once carried weight may over the years become clichés. "That they may all be one" (John 20:21) is an example of such a word. It is almost impossible to think of this saying of Jesus except as a recommendation for ecumenical action among the varying denominations. It has become a slogan, powerful in its own good way, to be sure, and has been stitched on more banners in more languages than any other word of Jesus in the twentieth century. But did Jesus foresee denominationalism and utter these words as an antidote? Is it possible that they originally had other uses?

Oneness is a central symbol in the Fourth Gospel and has a way of turning up in one guise or another from beginning to end. Jesus and the Father are "one" (John 10:30; 17:11), and Jesus prays that all who come to faith through the word may be "one" (17:20, 23). He has earlier in the Gospel exulted, "There will be one flock, one Shepherd" (10:16).

As John meditated long and lovingly on the cross of Jesus, he came to see oneness as a central yield of Jesus' death. The tradition had it that Jesus died for Jews and Gentiles, for the disciples and for generations yet unborn (17:20). In a passage near the end of his narrative of Jesus' ministry, John mulls over that tradition and adds that Jesus died not for the nations only, but "that all the scattered children of God might be gathered into one" (11:52).

Besides these passages that explicitly use the word "one," John reveals his interest in the theme of oneness in numerous other passages. In his telling of the feeding of the five thousand, John focuses loving attention on the gathering up of the leftover fragments. Jesus commands the gathering, the disciples do it, and it all happens "so that nothing may be lost" (6:12). Unbelief and distance from God are described as being lost or scattered also in other passages (3:16; 17:12; 18:9). The people of the world are like fragments of bread scattered among a great throng, like sheep scattered and lost on a thousand hillsides, like embers of fire dispersed on the ground and growing dim, like the tribes of Israel captive among the nations. People without faith are cut off from the generative and nurturing sources of their being in God.

Conversely, God's project in Jesus is described as gathering, saving, and uniting. The work of Jesus, consummated in cross and resurrection, bequeaths oneness upon people formerly scattered from God and lost in unbelief. That gift of Jesus is described parabolically in the incidents of the seamless robe (19:23–24) and the untorn net (21:8).

Jesus is the downward and outward movement of God, sweeping through an unbelieving cosmos. He descends to speak the truth of God with every breath and deed, and mounts up to God again by means of the ladder of the cross. In that coming down and going up again he calls and gathers people into his own upward motion, up from darkness and lostness, up from unbelief into the life of God. To dwell in God and to have God indwelling one's own life (cf. 14:23) is oneness.

When Jesus prays that his disciples may all be one, he asks that they may all live in God as Jesus also dwells in God (17:21–23). That means nothing less than to be filled with the glory of self-giving love. The glory of that love, binding the Father and Jesus and the followers of Jesus in oneness, is the theme of Jesus' prayer. When disciples truly are in God and are themselves suffused with the glorious life of God, then the world will be well and truly challenged to recognize Jesus as the agent of God. The world will come to know itself as cherished by God (17:23).

As the prayer draws to a close, and as his life on earth draws to its victorious close, Jesus prays that the disciples given to him by the Father may be with him, where he is (v. 24). Where is he? Where does he live and abide? Other parts of the New Testament like to describe the crucified and resurrected Jesus as exalted to "the right hand of God." John appears to have meditated on that image and finally to prefer related but different language: Jesus is forever "in the bosom of the Father" (1:18) or is simply "in God" (17:21). And when the disciples also are in God, what will they see? "My glory," says Jesus, "which thou hast given me in thy love for me before the foundation of the world" (17:24). The glory of Jesus is displayed forever in the cross, since the glory of God—the whole weight and substance of God—is *agape* or love. Father and Son are bound by such love from eternity to eternity.

The world is not righteous and that is the same as saying that the world is by definition "world" or cosmos. And it is that precisely because the world "has not known" God or the Son of God (v. 25; cf. v. 3). But disciples have passed from death to life and are no longer lost and scattered, because in Jesus they know and recognize the "name" of God, and that means the reality of God (v. 26). Disciples live in that name and reality. As he prepares to depart, Jesus vows that as he has made known the name of God, so he will continue to do (v. 26). He will continue to be a wellspring of knowledge, of enlightening energy, of transformative revelation. Jesus will continue to be God's "word" (1:1), conquering hearts and minds by the revelation of divine love.

When Jesus prays that the disciples may be "one," he is asking that the love binding Father and Son may spill over into disciples. Love is the powerful essence of God's life and God's glory. Celebrating Easter means embodying the love of God. It means being filled with the life of Jesus Christ (v. 26) and taking up the struggle against the corrosive forces of "the world." Those worldly powers divide from the life of God and set the peoples of earth against one another. Jesus Christ lived and died and rose again to bind us in oneness to divine, life-giving love.

The Day of Pentecost

Lutheran	Roman Catholic	Episcopal	Common Lectionary
Gen. 11:1–9	Acts 2:1–11	Acts 2:1–11 or Joel 2:28–32	Acts 2:1–21 or Gen. 11:1–9
Acts 2:1–21	1 Cor. 12:3b–7, 12–13	1 Cor. 12:4–13 or Acts 2:1–11	Rom. 8:14–17 or Acts 2:1–21
John 15:26–27; 16:4b–11	John 20:19 23	John 20:19–23 or John 14:8–17	John 14:8–17, 25–27

"Jesus promised the kingdom, but all that came was the church" (Alfred Loisy). That is an old and bitter complaint. It would be a simple matter to multiply complaints. But Pentecost is the "birthday" of the church, and birthdays are for celebrating and not for carping or criticizing. The church often fails to live up to its high calling, but today is a time to remember beginnings with gratitude. And it is a day to recover old promises.

The lessons for this festival focus on what happens in the aftermath of Easter. God breathes the Spirit of new life upon the world, and that creative inbreathing has varied consequences. Women and men are called into fresh allegiances (Acts 2). They become God's own dear children, crying, "Abba, Father," even in the midst of appalling suffering (Romans 8). Indwelt by the unworldly Spirit of truth, they have the promise that they will do "greater works" even than Jesus (John 14).

FIRST LESSON: ACTS 2:1–21

The Spirit descended upon Jesus at his baptism (Luke 3:22), upon the 120 Jerusalem disciples (Acts 2), upon Samaritans (Acts 8), upon

Saul/Paul (Acts 9), upon Cornelius and his household (Acts 10–11), and upon the Ephesian disciples (Acts 19).

Of all these "pentecosts," the Jerusalem Pentecost is narrated in especially impressive fashion: a sound burst forth like the rushing wind and what looked like tongues of fire played on each head, and they all began to speak in other tongues (2:1–4). People from far-away places could understand what the disciples spoke (2:5–8). The homelands of all those languages are named in the table of nations (2:9–11).

Why does Luke emphasize all those nations? Pentecost was originally an agricultural festival celebrating the offering of the first fruits of the grain harvest (Lev. 23:15–16). Did Luke intend readers to see the three thousand converts from all those territories and lands as the first fruits of a greater harvest yet to come? By New Testament times the Jewish festival of pentecost was connected with the giving of the law through Moses to Israel. Are readers to see parallels and contrasts between the Spirit and the Law as identity symbols of church and synagogue? Or is the table of nations and the narrative of the building of the tower of Babel (Genesis 10–11) lurking in the background? If so, then Pentecost indicates a fresh deed of God in these last times, one that removes the old curse and reunites the peoples of the earth.

Another parallel is less well-known but deserves consideration. Some ancient Jewish authors offered lists of nations as they made propaganda for the invincibility of Rome (and therefore for the futility of rebellion) or for the marvelous spread of Jewish religion (Josephus, War 2.358–89; Philo, Embassy to Gaius 8–10; 281–84).

In any case, Luke is declaring that God has now released energy sufficient to unite divided peoples in a universal kingdom of godly peace, under the lordship of Jesus Christ, raised from the dead and seated at God's right hand.

As he describes the first Pentecost, Luke portrays an ecstatic moment charged with pneumatic energy. At the same time, he carefully guards against misinterpretations of the Christian movement as frenzied or orgiastic. Some bystanders misunderstood the commotion. They heard only a kind of babbling and began to mock the apostles as early-morning drunkards. Luke, however, emphasizes that the outpouring of the Spirit resulted not in ranting or raving but in sensible and reasoned speech (cf. 1 Corinthians 14). Peter stood up and ridiculed the idea that wine was producing all the uproar (2:12–13). That speech in the language of all those nations was nothing less than the fulfillment of the vision of the prophet Joel (Acts 2:14–21).

Peter uses the apocalyptic images of Joel 2:28–32 in order to define the Pentecostal outburst as God's own gift at a decisive turning point in the history of humankind. In fact, that Pentecostal gift was not only prophesied by God but is decisive for the destiny of humankind.

Wherever church life is perceived to be dull and flat or uninspired, it is tempting to pray for the gift of the Spirit, hoping that the Spirit will produce some excitement. Sometimes Christians pray for any kind of excitement.

Luke reports that Pentecost was not mere excitement. He even avoids describing the moment the way Paul describes speaking in tongues (1 Corinthians 12—14). Both Luke and Paul are afraid that outsiders will misinterpret the work of the Spirit as some kind of emotional frenzy or madness. Luke is at pains to herald the good news that the first Pentecost both produced and promised a very particular kind of "madness"—the crossing of ancient boundaries and the binding of peoples into a new community under God. A loving community of persons united in spite of deep-seated barriers of race or class, nation or ideology is still the goal of the Spirit's working today.

SECOND LESSON: ROMANS 8:14–17

Both here and in Galatians 4, Paul contrasts being children with being slaves (cf. John 15:12–17). Through the life and death and resurrection of Jesus, God has raided the prison-house of the world and sprung the locks on the cages of religious institutions, political ideologies, and economic systems. God has breathed out the Spirit, quickening and liberating. God wants not slaves and slavishness but children (Rom. 14:15). And God would have the children live like pampered offspring, secure in the knowledge that they are loved.

Here in the heart of a letter penned in Greek, Paul uses an old Aramaic word. It is a homely word, one of the first words a Jewish child would learn in ancient times: *Abba* (v. 15). It means simply "Daddy" or "Papa." The word signals intimacy, familiarity, naturalness, and trust.

Ancient people avoided using this word in speaking to God and instead used much more reserved and formal speech like "our Lord," "our God," "King of the universe." Jesus used the intimate word of the most trusting relationship in his own address to God (Mark 14:36), sign of his unique sonship. But then he also taught his followers to use that same word *Abba* (cf. Gal. 4:6; Luke 11:2). He thereby invites his community to share in his own most intimate and blessed relationship with God.

As God's children, we are also heirs, God's heirs and inheritors together with Jesus Christ (v. 17; cf. Gal. 4:7). The great benefit we will inherit is glorious and glorified life. That new life in Christ and with God is ours, says Paul, "provided we suffer with him" (v. 17, RSV). The latter should be rendered (following Roy Harrisville), "if it is true (as it really is) that we suffer with him" (*Augsburg Commentary on the New Testament—Romans*, 1980). Paul does not make suffering a condition of inheritance. What he means is that closeness to God almost inevitably arouses the antagonism of the world. Suffering is the common experience of the children of God.

Suffering looks and feels like evidence against our status as children of God. Paul grants that Christians bleed and hurt, but he insists that they suffer neither alone nor hopelessly. Their suffering is "with Christ." With Christ and in Christ the children of God are headed for glory. They have God as "Abba-Father" now and they will in God's own good time receive their glorious inheritance.

Paul here wrestles with the age-old issue of innocent suffering. He handles this topic the same way he deals with every other issue: he takes it to the cross. In the cross he sees God involved in human pain and suffering, identifying with it and bearing it. God is not aloof but very near, as the word "Abba" already declares. If we are the intimates of crucified and resurrected Jesus, we are the intimates of God. And if we experience suffering as pressure from the world, as Jesus experienced that pressure, then that particular suffering (even if not all suffering) is the beginning of the experience of the life of the new creation. Then that particular suffering bears within it the promise of the inheritance of glory. This "glory" (v. 18) is the deliverance of the whole cosmos from its bondage to death and decay. We celebrate Easter whenever we throw off that bondage and know ourselves as God's free children, loving one another as Christ has loved us.

GOSPEL: JOHN 14:8–17, 25–27

On the eve of Jesus' departure from this world by death, Philip expresses anxiety about being cut off from Jesus and therefore being cut off from God. He and the others have basked in the sunshine of Jesus' presence and have no desire to be thrust back into darkness and the ice age of unbelief. He begs to be shown the Father in such a way that it will never again be possible for the disciples to be severed from their connection with God (John 14:8).

Philip's request betrays that he does not yet understand who Jesus is or what his dying means. Jesus is no mere teacher or prophet or sage. "He who has seen me has seen the Father," Jesus declares (v. 9). Jesus is in the Father and the Father in Jesus. God is present and energetic in all the words and works of Jesus (vv. 10–11).

And the death of Jesus is not the end but a glorious new beginning. He is not going into eternal darkness as the disciples fear. Exactly because Jesus goes by way of the cross to the Father, to the very heart of God, the connection between disciples and God will be closer than ever before. They will have unprecedented access to God through Jesus, and the power of God will flow out through disciples in astonishing and apparently unlimited measure. Followers of Jesus will do "greater works" than Jesus has done (v. 12)! Their works will be "greater" in geographical and chronological extent and will result in "greater" numbers of women and men coming to know God, just as Jesus prayed (cf. 17:20).

Jesus can speak in John's Gospel of the future, postcrucifixion connection between disciples and God both with and without reference to the Spirit. In John 14—16 Jesus speaks in five distinctive passages of the Spirit as Paraclete, Counselor, or Advocate (14:15–17; 14:26; 15:26–27; 16:7–11; 16:12–14). The Paraclete is a kind of alter ego of Jesus, the particular form of the presence of God after the exaltation of Jesus. The Paraclete has no fresh and independent mission but continues the mission of Jesus through the disciples.

In the present context the Paraclete is called "the Spirit of truth" (14:17), the divine power that snatches disciples from the jaws of the lie and the grip of the great liar (cf. 8:44–45). Jesus tells the truth and is the truth. And the Paraclete will dwell with Jesus' followers and in them forever (v. 17), destroying darkness and unbelief, opening their eyes, bringing them to faith, and binding them to God.

The weaponry of the Spirit-Paraclete is the record or narrative of the words and deeds of Jesus. The Spirit-Paraclete will bring that narrative to life in the lives of disciples. The Spirit-Paraclete, says Jesus, "will teach you all things" (v. 26). So Thomas (v. 5) and Philip (v. 8) and all the disciples may let their anxieties go, and rest unperturbed on the peace bestowed by Jesus. That peace is the solid connection between God and disciples forged by Jesus (vv. 25–27).